ARTHUR GILBERT

PRIME TIME

Children's Early Learning Years

Citation Press ∘ New York ∘∘∘ 1973

For reprint permission, grateful acknowledgment is made to:
Atheneum Publishers for "Outside" by Lillian Moore from
I Feel the Same Way, Copyright © 1967 by Lillian Moore.

Alfred A. Knopf, Inc. for *"The Dream Keeper"* by Langston
Hughes from *The Dream Keeper and Other Poems,* Copyright © 1932 and renewed 1960 by Langston Hughes.

Photographs by Ronald Gilbert

Cover and text design by Spring

To Carole
Gina
Jan
Robin
Ronnie
& Darcy

preface ○○○○○○○○○○○○○○○○○○○○○○○○○○○○○○○

This is a very personal book—a person-to-person sharing of the experiences of a "prime time" educator
whose school is firmly rooted in concern about "the
development of human qualities." The author invites
parents, teachers, neighbors—all those interested in
children—to join him in a search about which he
states: "In seeking roads to understanding, I do not
overlook the one that leads to my own door."

The vivid descriptions of an insightful observer, who
is at the same time a totally involved participant, open
the door wide on a learning environment rich in a variety of activities, experiences, and relationships shared
by three-, four-, and five-year-olds and adults who respect them. Few will be able to resist the invitation of
this open door, especially after they begin to meet the
children. Warmly introduced as growing, learning individuals, they interact with a purposefully prepared

environment unrestricted by rigid routines, inflexible time schedules, unreasonable expectations of performance, or walls that block exploration of the out-of-doors.

It is the children who make this book live. But through their stories adults can begin to formulate or expand their own learning about ways to contribute to the learning of threes, fours, and fives. Here they will find no set curriculum, no slavishly sequenced program, no "kits" of material, no short-cut drills to so-called academic success—in other words, no pat answers or panaceas. What they will find is an invitation to share and join the search for understanding with an educator who is excited by the adventure of the seeking.

Ruth Flurry
Chief, Bureau of Child Development
and Parent Education, New York
State Department of Education

thanks ○○○○○○○○○○○○○○○○○○○○○○○○○○○○○○○○○○

This book was begun at the suggestion of Dr. Charles S. Levy, a professor at the Wurzweiler School of Social Work, Yeshiva University. He criticized my first chapters and helped me discern what coverage would be most meaningful.

As the manuscript grew, Benjamin Siegel, the novelist, gave me another helping hand. He read the work in progress; pronounced it readable; and made a series of suggestions on how to move ahead.

Richard M. Radford, M.D., F.A.A.P. read the completed manuscript to assure its accuracy on pediatric concerns. In this and all during my school's existence his advice has helped us serve the whole child.

Our outdoor classroom evolved from suggestions made by Ruth C. Flurry, Chief of the Bureau of Child Development and Parent Education, New York State Education Department, and John D. Focht, Cooperative Extension Agent. Miss Flurry introduced me to the Adventure Playground. Mr. Focht taught me about and helped me cut our nature trails.

Mary L. Allison has given me reason to value a good editor. Her perception and skill enabled me to better say what I wished to say.

Arthur Gilbert

contents ○○○○○○○○○○○○○○○○○○○○○○○○○○○○○○

chapter 1 ∞∞∞∞∞∞∞∞∞∞∞∞∞∞∞∞∞∞∞∞

Do They
∞∞∞∞∞∞∞∞∞∞∞∞∞∞∞∞∞∞∞∞ Just Play?

"What I'm most interested in is that he learns how to get along with other children. He has time to start learning other things when he goes to elementary school."

"Do they really learn anything or do they just play?"

These are two questions nursery school teachers are often asked. Here are some others:

"Do you teach them anything? I mean, do you teach them numbers? Do they learn how to read?"

"What do you do if a child really is bad?"

"How do you discipline a child?"

These and whatever other questions parents ask are important. They help me understand what parents expect when they send their children to my nursery school. I listen carefully and try to answer with equal care. The questions tell me about the questioner and provide an excellent opportunity to clarify and inter-

7

pret. The parent who is interested only that her child "learns how to get along . . ." sees her child as less than he really is and views the nursery school in limited perspective as well. A child is indeed learning how to get along with others, but he is also learning more about the world around him than he will in any equivalent span of time later in life.

There is widespread agreement that the early years are the prime learning time. This should be understood because a child is interacting with other children and adults in situations that abound with learning opportunities. As for the effective nursery school, it is seen by many of us as fully as important in the educational spectrum as college or the professional school.

Inclusion of the modifier in the phrase "do they just play?" shows a lack of understanding of the values of play. Some people trained in early childhood education are beginning to shy away from the use of the word *play* because of some of the pressures now being applied to early learning. *Play* is, nevertheless, wonderfully descriptive of what the child does. While he plays, he learns. This is how he learns best. There are all kinds of play. Some are destructive. When a child torments an animal, crayons all over a wall, makes a hole in a wall, shoots toy guns, throws stones at passing cars, or steals pennies from a newsstand—he may be playing. These are but a few of the forms play takes in random situations where there is no suitable supervision.

Play in nursery school should be of the best kind, allowing for accentuating positive tendencies and eliminating the negative. Destructive acts occur in nursery school as they do elsewhere, but the teacher is able to stop some situations and uses others to help the child learn. There is certainly at least as much tendency for a child to want to learn what is worthwhile as to learn destructiveness. Not only do I believe this but I would further state that there is far more interest in creating than in destroying—if the play is relevant and meaningful to the child.

So when I am asked about discipline, I answer that we will scold a child when he deserves it and we will separate a child from play or playmates if he repeatedly violates others' rights or reasonable limits. We set reasonable limits (and evaluate to be sure they are legitimate) and we maintain them consistently and persistently. An observer seldom sees any unusual testing or any severe discipline.

Each of our classes has a serene feeling. Testing and problems are always there to be sure, but almost everyone who has seen them agrees that they are indeed serene. One lady described them as "too ideal." She was asked to come again to be sure that what she observed was not atypical. I work to create this serene feeling—it is there by design. I believe it to be appropriate for the young child. My classes are also stimulating—again by design. The children are obviously interested and absorbed in what they are doing. They are eager and responsible participants in their own little nursery school world.

My basic premise is to work with the whole child. That may sound ridiculous. Surely no one would propose that less than the whole child be taught in any school. Nevertheless, that is precisely the practice of too many teachers, and it also reflects the attitudes of too many parents as well. The all too prevalent attitude is that a child is sent to school to learn the three R's.

That, in effect, presumes that the brain is being filled with academic skills—each carefully poured in at the appropriate time and in a suitable manner by the teacher.

But what happens when a child comes to school with undiagnosed perceptual defects?

What happens when a child comes to school with defects of speech or is disinclined to use speech?

What happens to the overly dependent child when he comes to school?

What happens to the child who has never learned to play?

What happens to the overaggressive or the withdrawn child?

What happens to the child who lacks an adequate self-image or has a negative image of himself?

What happens to the child who has been taught to repress his feelings?

Or what happens to the child whose family life involves great stress from serious illness, death, financial problems, or other serious continuing troubles?

Such children can be found in many classrooms. I found them in day care classes when I directed a settlement house, in nursery classes when I directed a community center, and in almost every class I've seen, including those in my own nursery school. These represent only a few of the problems children bring into the classroom. Every child deserves his full measure of understanding. He is a complex being. He is intellect—emotion—body—soul—will. He is an individual. He is a social being. He is more than the sum of all these parts.

If a child has a perceptual defect, a teacher can see

that he is seated where he can see or hear well, and she tries to be sure to face him and speak distinctly. Her desire to reach each child through understanding and her ability to translate that understanding in her relationship with him are prime attributes of a good teacher. If we realize that the preceding listing of special needs of children is only a small fraction of the total, we may wonder whether a teacher can possibly tap the necessary resources to competently serve a full class of children. I believe she can—providing she knows what resources she has and uses them well. Some of the resources found within my classroom are:

The child himself is the most important resource. His ability to learn, to achieve, and to grow are essential to the teaching–learning process. His motivation and his drives need to be understood and nurtured.

A teacher's aide is capable of functioning in almost every role of a teacher. To maximize an aide's effectiveness, she should be given in-service training and be included in staff conferences concerning the children.

Classmates can teach many lessons. The problems they provide for each other are not likely to be found in even the most creative of lesson plans. Their abilities to understand and help each other often leaves a teacher shaking her head in wonderment.

The classroom should be regarded as a tool or facility for teaching. It includes the usual physical classroom space, equipment selected and placed in it, outdoor play areas, the equipment placed there, the surrounding ecosystems, and the places visited on trips.

Outside the classrooms there are other important helpful resources. Parents, for instance, can have much impact on their children's education if they fulfill their roles actively, consciously, and skillfully. When parent and teacher confer, they usually discover that each of them holds separate pieces of information that when fitted together give both a clearer picture of the child.

To establish the child's physical well-being his pediatrician or family doctor is a primary resource. Sometimes evaluation by other professionals may also be necessary.

As director I help through my work with teachers and parents. I also work directly with children in the classrooms. I am especially sensitive to their need to have more opportunity to enjoy the companionship of a man. There are not enough men in the classrooms of young children, many of whom do not spend adequate time with their fathers.

Robin Hill Nursery School opened February 1962 in an oversized house in Monsey, New York. It began with two classes. Mrs. Gilbert and I were the teachers. Within two years it grew to four classes, and we began seeking a location that would allow further growth. In 1965 I located a new site in nearby Suffern and built the present school. It now has eight classes, each staffed by a teacher and an aide.

In selecting an architect for the building, I sought one who would incorporate my ideas on education into his design. It took five tries before I found the right one. One I rejected told me, "Yours is the status school of this community." When I replied, "I don't see it that way," he insisted I was being too modest. Modesty had no part in my response. The connotations of "status school" are repugnant to my concept of a good classroom. My school has always had an open admissions policy. Children are registered on first-come, first-serve basis. I seek to have twenty different children in each class. Their differences reflect the diversity of the community. The diversity and the problems are essential parts of a good nursery classroom.

I immediately include parents as participants in this experience. At our first meeting we have an intake interview. This is intended to give parents an understanding of what we are trying to do, awareness of how we do it, examples of the process of the specific experiences through which teaching and learning occur, and preparation for specific roles parents fulfill in relation to the child's classroom experiences. Our discussion evolves from a statement of my objectives:

To provide a setting where children are encouraged to learn about themselves and others—explore their world—grow in curiosity—and develop their individual capacities.

The discussion is divided into two parts. First we talk about the implications of *learning about themselves and others:*

This describes essentially what happens as a child gains realization of himself as a social being. By trying out thousands upon thousands of pieces of behavior as he interacts with his playmates and his teachers, he gradually sorts out what is most comfortable and effective for him. He learns what he likes and dislikes about himself and about others as well.

Developmental studies show that experiences in social adjustment begin to occur at about the age of three. A child has progressed from the total dependency of early infancy through the egocentric period of late infancy. The borders of his world in those early years did not extend far beyond his fingers and toes. Mother was his first source of security—the doer of all good things—the satisfier of all his needs including feeding, burping, dressing, caressing. The solver of all his problems—was mother. It is easy to understand that he may tend to seek her out for more help as he encounters problems in school. She remains for some time the source of his security—the one he reaches for when the going gets rough.

As a child makes his first moves towards increasing his ability to function as an independent being, the wise mother recognizes that her roles are changing. If she functioned with reasonable effectiveness as the child moved through his infancy towards early childhood, she has already experienced the kinds of roles she will increasingly play as she changes from *the solver of all his problems* to *the enabler*. For an infant's first steps, the mother knows she must hold his hand, but she also knows she must let go at some point. The letting go is as important in this teaching–learning process as the holding on. She also knows that when she lets go, he will move with uncertainty; he will totter; he will stumble; he will fall; he will cry in dismay; but it is almost certain he will pick himself up again and persist and ultimately learn to walk. This description can be generalized to include other learning processes. Something new or unknown is tried; some solutions fail; some succeed; gradually the ineffective solutions are sorted out, the effective ones reinforce each other, and finally learning occurs. The relative impact of the successes and failures is not easily measurable, but there is no doubt that they are both essential contributors to learning.

The process of socialization in which a three-year-old learns how to get along with children and adults other than family will include a gamut of experiences far greater in range than that of learning to walk. He will begin to discover some of the many pleasures that are found in human relationships. Through his interactions and identification with other humans, he moves towards realization of himself. Along with the many

pleasures, he will also find problems. I am aware that most parents see some measure of their child's happiness coming from play with his classmates. It is indeed a major source. All too often, they make too little allowance for the actual problems he will encounter. I try to prepare them by saying, "In addition to the friendships he will make and the pleasures he will experience, his class will probably include children who bite—pinch—hit—scratch—scream—tease."

"I don't like you!"

"You're bad! I won't play with you!"

"If you let me play with your new toy, I'll invite you to my party."

"I'm gonna tell everybody you're selfish and nobody will play with you!"

These and similar remarks are heard daily by children and also by any adult who is interested enough to listen. They are seldom original, usually blunt, and designed to get immediate results.

As these physical and verbal encounters occur, as with tottering and falling when children learn to walk, the kids react and adjust and learn to live as part of a group. Many of those who boldly face their tormenting peers (and surely those who are not bold) earnestly look forward to their return home so they can unburden their souls to mother:

"I don't like Herbie. He always hits me!"

"You should see what Jamie did!"

"There are no nice children in my class."

"Nobody likes me! I don't have anybody to play with!"

A mother's empathy for her child will make her feel the pain of his hurts. But as a parent and/or as a teacher she needs to be aware that the most effective help she can give is to guide her child toward independence. She should know that the nursery school situations are the best forms of play that can be provided. The teachers and teachers' aides are there to help each child toward that same goal of self reliance. Knowing this, a parent can give his child the kinds of reassurances that will get him back to that classroom the next day, ready for the problems and pleasures that day will bring.

chapter 2 ∘∘∘∘∘∘∘∘∘∘∘∘∘∘∘∘∘∘∘∘∘∘∘∘∘∘∘∘

Exploring
∘∘∘∘∘∘∘∘∘∘∘∘∘∘∘∘∘Their World

Our classroom style is that of an open classroom. The effectiveness comes not so much from *what* is done, as from *how* it is done. Freedom of choice and movement are frequently misunderstood. Recently as I was discussing this with a principal of an inner-city school, he told me about a two-week-old open classroom. The first week everything worked. At the end of the second week, two of the students decided they would run around the room as though they were conducting a speed test on an obstacle course. The teacher then directed his efforts at moving them into learning situations and helping them understand some significant differences between license and freedom. In this situation the teacher knew what the kids were doing, and his own role was equally clear.

It is often not realized that while students in the traditional classroom sit at their desks with their workbooks in front of them, their minds are elsewhere. I remember a story told about the teacher who asked my mother to come to observe me in class. As the lesson proceeded, my eyes were fixed on the outdoors. "Now watch this," the teacher whispered to my mother and then suddenly asked a question about the lesson. I turned and gave her the correct answer. She slapped her hand emphatically on her desk. "That," she said in a tone of mixed anger and frustration, "is what I wanted you to see. It happens every time." I made my escape in daydreams that were far more interesting than her lesson plans, and yet by keeping one foot lightly planted in her world, I was able to carry out my passive resistance.

Our play experiences cover what is usually included under the heading of common branch subjects. Freedom of choice and movement make sense in terms of a child's abilities and attention span. The open classroom provides an optimum climate for the development of initiative and for providing opportunities that will help a child develop his ability to seek and find interest areas and follow through independent study. The early formative years of the traditional, tightly imposed curriculum may have served to thwart or destroy these capacities in many students.

In describing the second part of my statement of objectives I say during the intake interview, "This is our curriculum . . . *explore their world, grow in curiosity, and develop their individual capacities.*"

Some parents ask, "How can this be a curriculum? None of the usual subjects are mentioned."

The omission is intentional. It serves to emphasize that the child is my central concern. *Exploring* is exactly

what the three-, four-, or five-year-old is doing. If it happens to be autumn, an adult recognizes the coloration of the foliage, dried leaves on the ground, and trees becoming barren. There are many nuances: sounds such as the rustling of dried leaves as they are blown about by the wind, the sharp crackle of cold, dried branches as they snap underfoot, the absence of many birds and animals who are more active and more frequently seen and heard in summer and spring. A child looking at the same scene may be seeing for the first time in his life a change of seasons, and if one tries to view the world as he sees it, an adult soon realizes he is looking at an entirely new world. Furthermore, a child lacks years of experience and education to draw upon when he seeks to assimilate the new information.

All education is directed at teaching about the world in which we live, to increase our understanding of it, and our abilities to cope with it. Parents often ask whether we teach numbers or letters. My response is that we teach most of the usual subjects—reading, writing, arithmetic, and so on—but that each is taught in terms that have meaning for the three-, four-, or five-year-old.

Language is the most basic of all subjects. It is needed for oral communication and for reading and writing. Since oral or written communication is involved in almost every other course of study, language is the basic prerequisite of all further studies. Language development in the nursery school progresses in many ways. Group discussions, in various forms, take place several times each day. These include: Show and Tell, which allows each child an opportunity to speak about objects he has brought in or experiences he has had; clue games, which is our catchall name for a large variety of games that require different reasoning processes; word games; dramatic play; and singing. The many conversations that take place during play are also methodically observed and used as effective parts of the teaching–learning process.

The books that line the shelves of local libraries represent in that small space centuries of man's inspiration and thought that enable many of today's college graduates to be better informed than Descartes, Galileo,

Newton, and Copernicus. Our first task is to teach a child to love books. This we do by using books that are interesting, that deal with his special concerns, are well written and imaginatively illustrated. Not only are books used to inform and to reinforce experiences, but they transport him to new places or situations—and can also fill him with belly laughs. When we take a trip to a farm, for instance, we read about farms or farmers or farm animals. When we visit a large equipment plant, we read such books as *Katy and the Big Snow*.[1] (Katy is a crawler tractor, the workhorse of the highway department.) When spring approaches, we vicariously follow the little boy in *Hi Mr. Robin* [2] as he asks his grandfather and the postman and his mother to tell him whether spring will be coming soon.

People don't think we really teach math—or sometimes they think that we do on the assumption that we teach numbers and counting. Well, we earnestly do teach math, and though counting and systematic number thinking is a part of our concern, we are even more concerned with teaching the basic concepts: time, space, size, shape, quantity, location, and direction. Our task is better understood if one thinks of what most three-year-olds mean when they say yesterday. To them it is the vaguest of concepts. It connotes time —but nothing specific. It can mean anything from a few moments ago—back several years—or even a future event. Thus, we must direct our efforts to helping him understand that yesterday is a specific time. He needs also to learn about before, after, soon, now, morning, afternoon, evening, night, summer, winter, autumn, and spring. He need to know about more, less, some, all, bigger, smaller, taller, shorter, heavier, and lighter. We must patiently and resourcefully teach him. When he does understand these and many other concepts, numbers and symbols begin to have meaning for him, but until and unless he understands his basics, numbers and symbols are learned by rote and are therefore not really meaningful.

Some subjects frighten people. Every now and then someone will turn on a fatuous grin and ask, "Does your curriculum include sex education?"

I am tempted to reply, "Need you ask?" It is difficult to see how it could not be included. Procreation is not just a fact of life—it is a common occurrence. A look around the classroom at the children's art works is likely to reveal its presence. When a child's mother is pregnant, he may draw or paint his impressions of her condition. Ian did both. His pictures usually included his entire family, and his mother was easily distinguished because she had a figure drawn horizontally across her belly. In contrast to Ian's primitive style, Sally depicted this same condition in mod technique by drawing her mother's abdomen as a series of concentric circles.

A change in a child's behavior sometimes signals the mother's condition. A worried mother's call is another common occurrence, "How is Glen behaving at school? We're having quite a time with him at home. I think he's upset because I'm going to have a baby."

To fail to see this mother's need for reassurance would be a callous turning away from responsibilities to this parent-child and teacher relationship. I am concerned about the parent and equally concerned about the child. Much impress has been made on today's young parents about the impact of pregnancy and birth on the young child. In all too many instances they are left in limbo—worried—but not knowing what to do. I begin by lending my ear to allow the worried mother opportunity to express her concerns. My responses are directed at reassuring her by helping her realize that she and her child are in the midst of one of life's most rewarding experiences.

From the beginning of a child's interest in sex we make it clear that this is an open topic. Parents and school are ideally the two principal sources of information for the young child; they should be regular participants in his inquiries and this should continue as he matures. Their function grows in importance when we consider that many random sources of sex education include some that equate sex with smut.

As the teaching–learning process unfolds, facts relating to sex constantly come within the purview of our curricula. One concern stands out above all else—we do our best to create the attitude that views sex as beautiful, creative, normal, and desirable.

In trying to do this, parents and teachers should be conscious of their significance as key figures in a child's process of identification. To most children, mother is the first example of woman and father the first example of man. From the day-to-day relationship of his parents and the other adults he regularly sees, the child forms his identifications of and with the two sexes. The way these people speak to one another, the tenor of their relationship, the presence or lack of consideration, their reasonableness or unreasonableness, and their thoughtfulness or thoughtlessness serve as his primary lessons about man and woman.

A child looks at himself as a first source of learning

material. He then looks at his peers for comparison. He quickly realizes boys and girls are different. The topic should then be open. One way we make clear our intent is the toilet procedure. The door remains ajar, and the children use it freely and casually. Accidents are treated matter-of-factly. We change the child's clothing and send his home in a bag. Some mothers call, disturbed when this happens. I reply that this is something we expect and that such situations are handled to avoid embarassing the child. Instead of using the common euphemisms for two bodily processes we simply use the words urinate and defecate.

Living and growing things are given much attention during the school year. Outdoor play allows for much exploration. Indoors we talk, read, and sing about our experiences. Millicent Selsam's *All Kinds of Babies* [3] tells and shows how some baby animals look like their parents while others, such as the tadpole and caterpillar, begin quite differently and evolve to maturity as frog and butterfly respectively. *What's Inside* [4] is illustrated by an excellent series of stop-action photographs of the hatching of a goose egg, the first moments of its life as a gosling, and finally a shot of goose, gander, and gosling. *How Puppies Grow* [5] shows and describes the first few weeks of the life of six little puppies. We have an SVE series on animal babies showing in six separate film strips: *Mr. and Mrs. Robin and Their Springtime Family, Mr. and Mrs. Mallard and Their Family, Mrs. Squirrel and Her Family, Mrs. Cottontail and Her Springtime Family, Mr. and Mrs. Beaver and Their Family,* and *Mrs. Bear and Her Family.* [6]

We are particularly lucky to be able to observe the first four of these families right in our own setting. We want a child's foundation in sex to be as well prepared as in reading, writing, or arithmetic. As always, we first try to understand where he is in his thinking and then try to move him at a pace that allows him to assimilate new learning. Because the wrappers have been kept on sex education until recently, there may be a temptation to cover too much too soon. The feeling we convey is a most important factor at this time. A child's questions are not usually difficult to answer. We try to give answers that are factual and simple. I stress simplicity because over-explanation often introduces concepts that confuse children and cause misapprehensions.

It is wise to distinguish between discussions that can best be handled with an individual and ones that are suitable for group discussion. Before giving answers to questions, it sometimes is wise to be sure you are aware of the child's frame of reference. Sometimes he will answer his own question, if you direct it back at him. If you have at least some idea of this thoughts, you can appropriately fill in the blanks.

Knowing the importance of careful observation, recording, and evaluation, we have tried various means to achieve effective methodology. In my school there are no written tests, reports, projects, or compositions, nor are there psychological or educational evaluation tests. Despite the lack of all these, we have many opportunities to individualize and have developed much skill in seeing each child as an individual and working with him in terms of his specific needs.

Systematic observation and record keeping is our most effective device. Each teacher makes an anecdotal note on each child in her class at least once every five days. Teachers meet with me to discuss each child. Parents are advised or consulted whenever a need arises. Goals and working approaches or methods are established for each child on the basis of these observations and discussions.

Even at their crudest, the anecdotals are effective. When one teacher described a child as "a looker," we tried to see whether he was looking at particular children or at some kind of play or toy. We found we could often discern the apparent interest of a child and then try ways of helping him move into relationships or into specific kinds of play. This enabled us to help this child in ways that were responsive to his seeming desires rather than by a series of wild guesses. The anecdotals raise a series of questions that make us look more and more carefully at each child. We find ourselves comparing notes on each child, and by involving each staff member who has contact with each child and his parents, we find we are getting a clearer picture of each child and can therefore work more effectively.

Sometimes a parent asks me to describe a typical nursery school day. I answer that the usual day includes attendance taking, discussion, indoor free play, storytime, musical activity, snack, dressing, and outdoor free play. The routines themselves do not have great meaning. They can be understood better if one sees what happens to a child as he takes part in these activities.

Dressing and undressing, when seen from this viewpoint, becomes far more significant. Lacing boards, button boards, and beads and strings were all designed to help the young child learn to manipulate. These and many other devices provide the kinds of exercises a child needs as he develops small muscle skills and eye-hand coordination. He will need to refine these skills to be able to learn to write. His own clothing may possibly be the best of devices for this practice, provided teacher and parent are aware of it. Several times each day he is confronted by his own buttons, zippers, buckles, and laces as well as many articles of clothing. If, instead of reaching out our anxious hands to help him, we let him do for himself, he will have just so many more opportunities to practice and acquire the needed skills. This is why I encourage parents to be delighted when a child comes home with sweater inside out and buttoned out of line. "Be delighted," I say, "because he has put it on himself and he has buttoned it."

It would be wise for each of us to recall some of our own first tries at any piece of learning. Most of us can remember how much we appreciated a parent's or teacher's forebearance of our first crude efforts.

Parents earnestly seeking to nurture children's talents sometimes begin them on regimens of music, art, and dance lessons at the least glimmering of promise and at sacrifice of time and money. But they and their children's teachers tend to see creativity in a narrow frame of artistic endeavor and ignore other aspects. In today's world there is an increasing trend toward development of skills. Feelings, desires, relationship factors, and other human qualities are given attention only when they infringe upon academic concerns. "You're a big boy now," is heard more and more as a child ages. That phrase would be fine if it didn't often translate as,

"I'm not concerned about your human needs. Just see that you get your work done!"

Erikson makes a similar observation in *Childhood and Society* when he summarizes differences in nurture between the Sioux Indians and the mainstream of American society:

> In contrast, the dominating classes in Western civilization . . . have been guided by the conviction that a systematic regulation of functions and impulses in earliest childhood is the surest safeguard for later effective functioning in society. They implant the never-silent metronome of routine into the impressionable baby and young child to regulate his first experiences with his body and with his immediate physical surroundings. Only after such mechanical socialization is he encouraged to proceed to develop into a rugged individualist. He pursues ambitious strivings, but compulsively remains within standardized careers which, as the economy becomes more and more complicated, tend to replace more general responsibilities. The specialization thus developed has led this Western civilization to the mastery of machinery, but also to an undercurrent of boundless discontent and of individual disorientation.[7]

Because my school is concerned about the development of human qualities, as much attention is directed at observing and enhancing these as in helping children develop academic skills. Organizing our classes in vertical or family groupings is one effective method. In setting up classes, children are distributed in a two-year age spread. This tends to provide a wider range in individual skills and development than classes that have a one-year age spread. Much opportunity for free interaction between children is the concomitant method.

These two practices make an effective environment for teaching and learning and for personality development. The children's effectiveness in helping each other is greatly increased. Having recently passed through a particular phase of learning enables one child to understand the problems that confront another who is on the threshold of a similar learning experience. He can often sense and express what means the most at that particular point. This provides an additional source of help for the child who learns, *and* the child who helps gains as well. He is able to experience the role of a helping individual, and after he does that often enough, it becomes a facet of his personality. It also reinforces his own learning, when he teaches others.

chapter 3 ∘∘∘∘∘∘∘∘∘∘∘∘∘∘∘∘∘∘∘∘∘∘∘∘∘∘

The Child and
∘∘∘∘∘∘∘∘∘∘∘∘∘∘His Playthings

I stood next to four-year-old Tina and asked, "How tall are you?" She moved her hand from the top of her head to my thigh and said, "That tall," pleased at having expressed herself so well. I then asked her playmate how big his hand was. "That big," he replied, holding his palm against mine. Whenever I ask two children, "Which of you is taller?" they stand back to back and measure with the familiar hand maneuver.

It is axiomatic of good teaching to begin where the child is. The cue is clear. The way Tina and the others involved themselves physically in measuring is typical of three-, four- and five-year-olds. By constantly comparing himself with others around him, a child forms his first standards of measurement. Others include anyone conveniently near when questions are raised. Mother, father, sisters, brothers, playmates, and teachers are used constantly. The child is clearly telling us he should be included as a logical source of teaching material.

Using a child as teaching material not only enables teachers to know him better but also permits him to gain the awareness of self that everybody needs. Perhaps it will carry even further and give him useful knowledge of himself, of his capabilities and weaknesses, and how he compares with his peers. To encourage this self-awareness we often begin with guessing games, giving clues that identify individual children

in different ways: by their features, hair color, hair style, size, weight, or special aspects such as eye-glasses or a bruise or bandage. Clothing provides much material (if you will pardon the pun). Where or how a child is sitting or what he is doing sometimes makes a good clue.

A good math teacher would discern that such games provide material for many lessons. Feature and size comparisons and the many elements of clothing design are wonderful for teaching size and shape. When a child is learning what a circle is, his learning can be said to be well-rounded when he can identify the circle in the iris or retina of the eye, in the frames of someone's glasses, in the belt that goes around him, in a ring, in an earring, a button, in some head shapes, in many parts of clothes designs and patterns, or in a special way of holding thumb and forefinger.

Bigger, smaller, fatter, thinner, heavier, lighter, taller, and shorter are some of the size concepts that can be developed. Modes of measurement come into play and different ways tried. Lines on a wall marking the height of each child is a good introduction to measuring instruments.

In these games the teacher alters her roles constantly. She must adjust to each individual to allow for the range of differences in skills and understanding. Often she moves into the role of observer, giving the full direction of the play to the children.

Watching Mrs. Rosenthal's class play its version of a clue game is a treat. They form a circle, and the person in the center describes some characteristic of one of the other children. They play this in many variations. The characteristics can be random or sometimes follow a particular pattern. The children have considerable awareness of each other, and their clues show it. Mrs. Rosenthal and Mrs. Lawrence are as likely to find themselves in the center of the circle as anyone else. Mrs. Rosenthal is just five feet tall. Her tiny frame and her soft voice are the physical features of this skilled teacher who has much compassion. Mrs. Lawrence also has this quality. She adds merriment to our days with her frank perceptions stated in her English accent laced with British slang.

Hilda, a sweet, gentle child, who always speaks softly and perceives all sorts of things, especially small bits of wonderment, noticed her friend off in an obscure corner and said, "I see six gold buttons." It took a while, but David guessed it was Eileen, who sat apart from the others and was wearing a sweater that had three bright gold buttons on each sleeve.

Sometimes the games describe personality factors, as when Mrs. Rosenthal was *it* and said, "I'm thinking of someone who has a wonderful smile and knows a lot about birds." It was guessed immediately—David was the class authority on birds.

It is interesting, enlightening, and delightful to listen to them and discover how much they know about each other. Often their insights add significantly to the teachers'.

Ruby, a four-year-old who could neither see nor speak, put her hands on her nose, head, ears, and tummy while playing Simon Says. Her teachers then realized she could identify her own features and had at least this much self-awareness.

Here and there, between, at the end, far, from, near, in front of, behind, and next to are location concepts that must inevitably come into play as the children interact. If we are aware of the young child's need to learn and to clearly understand these concepts, we can find an endless source of effective lessons in their play.

A second source of material for teaching and learning is the immediate environment. As the untrained eye looks around the nursery school classroom, it sees many play opportunities. The trained eye sees much more. In each play area it sees rich resources for many learning experiences. A careful look at a nursery classroom will help reveal some of these opportunities.

Hortense Jones, the Director of the More Effective School Program of the New York City school system, tells a story [1] about an elementary school principal participating in a workshop on early childhood education that shows how even professionals may not be aware of the teaching potential of play materials.

"Do you really teach them or do they just play with blocks?"

"I'm glad you asked that question," answered Mrs. Jones. "Tomorrow I'd like each of you to come dressed so that you can sit on the floor and play with blocks. The entire session will be used as a block play workshop. Perhaps that will enable us to better understand how playing with blocks helps to effectively educate the young child."

The next day the administrators arrived in class appropriately attired. Mrs. Jones wasted no time. She pointed to the block case and told them to go to it. They moved, overly self-conscious, to the blocks. Their play was much like that of a group of three-year-olds. Each took a bundle of blocks, moved to his own niche, and built some small structure. They talked baby talk with each other to heighten the effect of young children at play. After about half an hour they were floundering badly. Their ideas on block play had run out.

Mrs. Jones called them together. She helped them evaluate their first lesson:

"The baby talk was not necessary. You are in the process of discovering how children learn from block play. You are also about to discover that adults, too, can learn from it. Your play just now was like that of a beginning group of three-year-olds. The first comparable quality was the complete lack of interaction. Each of you took a bundle of blocks and built your own structure. Interaction is a major factor in good block play. As children interact, they assume all sorts of roles and act them out. They are architects, engineers, builders, truckmen, road builders, creators of all sorts of imaginative structures. They are constantly exchanging roles—now supervisor, now worker. By your failing to interact, you proved that even mature adults do not easily move into such relationships. The lack of imagination you showed tells me that my role as teacher should enable you to use a little more of your potential and especially more imagination."

A discussion followed in which they conceived a plan to build a rough facsimile of the area surrounding the school where their workshop was being held.

They began again. This time they interacted. They assumed roles. They argued. They agreed. They gradually built their representation. As they did, Mrs. Jones worked with them as a nursery teacher works with her class. She moved amongst them, listening and talking, complimenting one for his imagination or ingenuity, occasionally underlining a piece of learning. She walked over to the principal who had asked the question that motivated the workshop.

"Is that a bridge?"

"Yes."

"Where is the river?"

He looked at the surrounding structures and discovered the logical location of the river and then moved the bridge to its proper place.

"How does a car cross your bridge?"

This required a rather elaborate explanation because his bridge had been built without a ramp and the car had to make a ninety degree climb to reach the bridge roadbed. As they talked, he decided a ramp would be a more practical approach.

The administrators gained new insights into the values of block play as a result of this experience.

Whenever I look at the block case, I'm reminded of that story. I'm reminded too that how little or how much one finds in the nursery classroom depends on the know-how the teacher brings with her. One teacher thinks they just play with blocks, and it is likely that little more than that occurs in her classroom. Another realizes that thousands upon thousands of learning experiences can come from that block case, and that is just what happens in her classroom.

As children interact, they assume roles. As they assume a role, they gain insight into that role. A supervisor gives orders and quickly discovers that his workers do not snap-to like devoted slaves. He may begin to learn something of the relative value of request and command. And while these and other factors of role-playing and relationships are being tested, language

and concept learning are taking place. As structures are conceived and built, the parts must be selected and placed. Just as the principal experienced some learning about the ramp or inclined plane, so does a nursery child learn to identify blocks by calling out size and shape comparisons. He learns by necessity that language is far more effective than hand gestures in identifying the different sized and shaped blocks and in designating their locations. Piaget must smile in satisfaction at the thought of block play, for not only is the young child building the layers of experience that are essential to real learning, but as he handles the blocks he is literally absorbing such learning kinesthetically through his fingertips as well as through ideational processes.

When observing many classrooms, over and over again I have noted how the understanding and skill of the teacher makes the difference between a sterile or a rich experience. From one observation of a school that had been extravagantly praised in a recent best seller on education, I disagreed with the author. The block case of the kindergarten class was one of the discrediting factors. It was located along a twelve-foot wall. Right in its middle, as if to divide it in half, was a wooden box that served as the home for the class guinea pig. Less than four feet from each side of the divided case was a long table. Between the abode of the guinea pig and the two long tables, all the potential block building space had been preempted. The cases filled with blocks indicated the teachers' awareness that blocks were appropriate play material for young children, but the manner in which they were placed in that room showed that they didn't know how to use them. In any effective nursery or kindergarten, blocks are located away from traffic and the case opens out on a good expanse of clear floor space. Wheel toys, human and animal figures, furniture, tubes, cans, lattices, and other materials should also be included as part of the block play equipment.

chapter 4 ○○○○○○○○○○○○○○○○○○○○○○○○

Including
○○○○○○○○○○○○○○○○○○○○○○○○○○○○ Parents

"I can't play in the sandbox. My mother doesn't like me to get sand in my shoes."

"Well I can. My mother doesn't care if I get dirty."

Multiply this conversatiion by infinity and you will realize how often parental attitudes are carried into school. As I watch children at play, I get glimpses of their family experiences. Their house-play daddies and mommies reflect impressions of their real parents. Some are warm and loving, some scold, and some are punitive.

This carry-over can be seen in almost every kind of play. Art works are often essays on family experiences. (Some are commissions for display in the homes of grandparents.) Block play reconstructs highlights of trips taken with parents. Discussions are punctuated by illustrations drawn from home. Their "me toos" re-inforce the impress of the discussion.

Feedback from parents clearly shows that this goes two ways. School events and attitudes constantly come out again at home.

Recognizing this interrelationship, I seek to make the most of it by working with parents. I sometimes call this an exercise in letting the right hand know what the left hand is doing. My first meeting with parents is the intake interview. This takes place during the year preceding a child's starting school. The agenda of this first meeting is a discussion of my school's objectives: To provide a setting where children are encouraged to learn about themselves and others—explore their world—grow in curiosity—and develop their individual capacities.

Some consider this a discussion of educational philosophy. Insofar as I do seek to underline the truths behind the objectives, it is philosophy. Its major thrust, however, is to present a clear picture of the specifics of the nursery school experience. This gives parents the kind of information and understanding that should be given working partners.

When making this appointment, I give a brief description of the interview, and as part of the instructions, the parent is asked to separate from his child when they arrive at school. The child goes to one of the classes while the parent talks with me in the office. There is sometimes a reaction:

"Is this really necessary at this time?"

"I'm not sure Helen is ready yet. After all, she'll be almost a year older when school begins."

"I don't see the point in this."

"I have strong feelings about forcing John to separate."

"You know Herbert might have a bad reaction. Don't you think that will have a bad effect on the school experience and make it more difficult for him."

These are but some of the phrases I have heard many times. I respond to whatever is said to make clear that I view the separation at the beginning of school as one that is relatively simple. It is comparable to a parent separating from his child at a birthday party. If I use this comparison, I am often told that many children won't leave their mothers at birthday parties. This I knew long long ago, for not only have I seen many a tearful ritual at school, but I've also seen, firsthand, tearful birthday party separations. My approach with my own children was always to carefully make sure that they were being left in good hands and under good circumstances, and, satisfied that was so, I departed.

I can well remember leaving my oldest daughter at one of her first birthday parties. After making sure she would be well taken care of, I was delayed in my departure by the mother of a good friend. A grandmother, she was impressed with how I had gone about leaving my daughter and felt impelled to express her feelings about what was happening. She thought it distressing and disgusting the way some of the young mothers carried on with their children.

"They've read too many books," she declared. "You know I've read as many books as they have," and she continued on for some time describing how she handled situations with her own children, including a hair-raising description of how she had thrown her daughter into a lake with instructions to sink or swim. Her daughter, a dear friend, has many fine qualities, but also has many anxieties and is asthmatic as well. As the mother's stories unfolded, I pictured her daughter going through a series of childhood ordeals.

My own view of separation is not at all like that of the grandmother. I think the sink or swim alternative is unnecessarily cruel, but separating from my child at the birthday party was a good circumstance. There are, of course, some parties that I would not take my children to.

That some children cry or that others act out tantrums when they separate is understandable. They want it known that they don't want to separate, and this is how they express their feelings. They need reassurance. They need to learn that they can separate and that people other than mommy are kind and good and fun, and this, like so much else, is learned most effectively when it is experienced. The reassurance a mother gives when she says, "Everything will be all right. No one will hurt you. Look, see all the nice children," do not really become reassurance unless she leaves and lets the child discover she is telling the truth. If she fails to let go, the child has good reason to conclude that she too is afraid. Her reassurances boomerang because they have been empty words, and she herself has not demonstrated enough courage or confidence to leave.

Here again is an opportunity more than a problem. There are so many good features in the nursery school, it is sheer waste not to use them properly. A child is able to experience a separation in excellent circumstances with people who care a great deal for the welfare of children and are trained to translate their concern into action.

Our failures in this area have been caused by parents

who could not or would not cooperate. I opened my school in the middle of a school year, and many of the children who came at that time "couldn't make it" or had been told they "weren't ready." They were school dropouts at age three. My education on separation began the day we opened our doors and has shown no sign of stopping.

At the beginning we had two modes of trial separation. In one, a parent stayed in school and moved out gradually. In the other, the first month was treated as a trial period, and at the month's end the parent decided whether the child would continue. One interesting discovery made during this period was that all the separation failures were with parents who insisted on staying or with those who wanted us to be sure we understood that there was a month's trial period. After our second year, I decided to eliminate both practices.

The trial period that ends in failure serves to reinforce the dependency relationship between parents and children who most need to succeed. For some odd reason I keep remembering one of the experiences that helped persuade me to change to our present practice. This trial separation failed at the end of one month. The child, a cherubic four-year-old, had been adjusting well. The mother refused to believe that. Several times each week she asked me, "How is Pauly doing?" When I said he was doing all right, she looked at me in disbelief. At the month's end she said she felt, "Pauly just isn't ready" and terminated his school experience. I saw Pauly and his mother in their neighborhood many times after that, and always his little fist was tightly clutched to her skirt.

Mother love and smother love are too often confused. The notion of indispensability is a hazard. That the mother is a special person is surely true. To help her child learn that he need not be afraid to move out into the world is one of her most important functions.

Our intake discussions help parents who have separation difficulties. They are helped towards a better understanding of how to function, *and they are asked to practice so that the child can experience a number of good separations before school begins.* Some parents ask if they can visit school with their children before the school year begins. If that is reassuring, I ask them to do so.

For those few children who continue to be insecure, there is no magic formula. The true magic is our belief in the child and in ourselves, and our willingness to try our best to help that child learn that we care for him and believe in him. We give such a child extra attention and much tender loving care. We don't push him into activities or insist that he play with the other children. We let him move at his own pace, and we try to learn what makes him comfortable and what upsets him. Then we try to move him towards those things that he seems to enjoy and help him over some of the rough spots.

○ THE DUET
One year began with a perfectly tearless Monday. Tuesday morning also was gloriously dry and cheerful. Tuesday afternoon there was a concert. Four children, all in the same class, cried in four-part harmony. Two

stopped within minutes. The other two continued a sporadic duet for about a half-hour. One then stopped, calmed down, and moved into play as though nothing had happened. Within the first hour of the afternoon the mother of this child appeared with a look of panic on her face. "Is Linda all right?" she asked. "Yes," I responded, "why don't you watch her through the one-way mirror."

After she watched for about fifteen minutes, the mother turned, incredulous, saying "I wouldn't believe it if I hadn't seen it." Then she explained that Linda had never separated from her, that she refused to stay with her grandmother, who lived in their home, and even refused to stay with her father.

During this conversation Charlotte, the girl who had continued to cry, was sitting in my office. Her crying stopped as soon as I took her out of class. She was quite happily visiting with me and seemed to enjoy my company. Linda's mother left, and I picked up the phone and called Charlotte's mother, Mrs. Roux. I had known Mrs. Roux six years. Charlotte's two older brothers had attended my school. Mr. Roux was a high school teacher and part-owner of a summer camp.

When I told Mrs. Roux what had happened, she said, "That was exactly what I expected. We had a terrible time with her at camp this summer. She attached herself to Mr. Roux or to me and followed one of us around all day, refusing to join her group."

This helped me understand Charlotte's enjoyment of my company. "I'm glad I called," I answered. "Now I realize that I had better cut the cord." I excused myself, took Charlotte back to her class, left her crying, and returned to the phone to tell Mrs. Roux what I had done. Leaving her alone was exactly what she wanted me to do.

Charlotte continued to whine quite a bit each day for the next two weeks. Each day it subsided slightly. In the third week her adjustment improved, but whines recurred with any change in routine. By the end of the month her adjustment was adequate; by the end of the year it was excellent. At the beginning of the next school year she began to cry all over again. This time it stopped before Wednesday of the first week. A new teacher, a new year, and Charlotte's fear of change showed itself again, but this time all of us—the teacher, Mrs. Roux, Charlotte, and myself—were armed with more knowledge of Charlotte's ability, and within days she was her usually happy self.

Linda, the other member of the duet, cried no more.

The mother who doesn't credit her child with a normal amount of courage and judgment can thwart this separation process. As I gave her intake instructions, Mrs. Wyner said, "I have strong feelings about forcing a child to separate." I insisted that she would have to agree to have her son go to a class. She finally did—after much discussion. She came to school on a hot summer day. She left her son in her car and came to my office to resume her pleading for a special mode of separation. We argued for half an hour. Then I looked out the window at the child, who was sweltering inside the hot car and crying at the top of his lungs. "Don't you think it would be better for him to play outside with the other children than to stay in that hot car," I suggested.

"I'll try," she replied, "but I don't think he'll play with them."

She took the overheated, crying child from the car. No time was spent washing off the perspiration. The tears were wiped, and before the sobs subsided she asked, "Do you want to play with those children?" The crying started up again. Mrs. Wyner closed out the interview. As she moved off she remonstrated, "You see, I knew this would happen."

The choice of confining a child in a hot car rather than separating to let him play with children is strange indeed.

If a child goes home and spends much time with adults other than his parents, I encourage the parents to relate pertinent information to these other adults, and whenever possible they are included in conferences. Grandparents, aunts, baby sitters, and housekeepers have taken part in such conferences. The presence of parent substitutes allows them to relate information and insights that add to our understanding of the child. They also participate in the formulation of our approach to working with a child, and this, too, adds to our combined effectiveness.

Knowing all the answers is impossible. Knowing enough to ask good questions compensates for a fair measure of our ignorance. When my teachers are puzzled, they question me. In turn, when I am puzzled, I question them. Sometimes we put our questions directly to a child, and he tells us what we need to know about him. We, of course, use reference books and resource people. Often parents come up with helpful answers. Sometimes a light turns on when parent and teacher converse.

I commented to a parent about cuts on her child, "She has some beautiful raspberries on her arms and legs."

"Yes," replied the mother. "She always seems to be falling over something."

"Maybe she needs an eye examination."

My postulation made sense to the mother. She took the child for an eye examination, and corrective glasses were prescribed.

In a somewhat similar situation I mentioned to a mother that "Herbie is constantly tripping over his own feet."

"Oh my goodness!" the mother exclaimed, laughing as she spoke, "I should have told you about that. You see he has wide feet, and it is difficult to get the proper width in his size, so we have to get him shoes that are a few sizes larger."

An odd series of changes in the behavior of a boy prompted me to call his mother.

"I'm puzzled," I said. "George has been doing some things lately that do not make sense to us. He knocks over blocks. He is forever jumping off something or other. He tries to get his friends to play as though they are fighting and he always has to win. And what is most puzzling of all, he has been taking off his outer clothing while he is riding on the school bus."

The call was made in mid-winter.

"He seems just fine at home," the mother replied.

Then she mused, "Only one thing puzzles me. . . . He's on a Superman kick."

"That's it," I answered. "That's the answer to our riddle. Superman knocks his fist through walls, Superman jumps up and flies, he is invincible in battle and is forever having to remove his outer clothing as he assumes his identity as Superman."

We laughed at having overlooked something so simple. George had completely perplexed us by failing to announce that he was playing Superman.

Communication is a big word nowadays. I would qualify it by adding such considerations as willingness to communicate, accessibility of communicants, and desire to listen and understand as well as to speak.

I remember a particularly long attempt at relating some information to a mother, who constantly sidetracked the conversation, going off into long-winded, irrelevant tangents. Finally she came up for breath and observed, "I know I talk a lot. Everybody tells me I do. I'll bet you don't think I understood what you were trying to tell me."

That was her most perceptive comment. I had earnestly tried to reach her but had given up long before she made that comment.

She might be classified with a group called *the impossible ones.* The common characteristics of this group are that the children have apparent problems, and so do the parents, but the parents are either unable, unwilling, or unready to recognize and deal with the problems.

In some instances, we are able to reach a child without the help of parents. Occasionally our effectiveness is better than we could reasonably expect. Even then, though, we remain apprehensive about the child's future. The likelihood of his being eventually affected by his parents' problems is great.

Referral to specialists is difficult. Many of today's attitudes toward mental illness are holdovers from the Dark Ages. Fear of being stigmatized deters people from seeking help that could mean the difference between living a satisfying life or one filled with fears, tensions, and anxieties. Some few parents are ready because they have developed enough insight to be aware that they have a problem. Some can accept a referral of their child but reject participation in the subsequent therapy or counselling. Some psychiatrists will not work with a child unless the parents are involved. Others are willing to begin alone with a child but usually need the parents' involvement as the treatment progresses. Despite the earnest efforts of many of us who take part in the helping processes, the largest segment of unsolved problems are the problems of mental health.

One novel approach I have tried has been effective in helping some people. I have taken a leaf from the approach of Alcoholics Anonymous and referred parents who have a problem to other parents who have had some success in solving the same kind of problem. This mode of helping has been acceptable to some who could not otherwise be reached. In most instances, it has proved helpful. In some, it has been exceptionally effective. I try to make careful selections when I make these referrals. Fortunately I am able to make my choices from a large group, including those who now have children in school and those whose children have been here in years past. There tends to be sensitivity and empathy in the conversations between parents who have experienced in the same kinds of problems. Their ability to identify with each other gives them insights that enable them to be of help to one another.

The possibility that their child may have any defect is crushing to some parents. Getting them to take the child to a pediatrician takes much effort. In many instances, an examination turns up simpler findings than were anticipated. Even when there are serious findings, early detection increases the possibility of remedy and avoidance of complications.

Inaccessability can be a problem. Anyone who has had reasonable experience in making referrals knows that some of these languish because of a combination of red tape, lack of facilities for performing the required services, or just plain carelessness.

When trying to find an appropriate next setting for Ruby, the multiply handicapped child, we ran into difficulty every way we turned. One agency insisted on a complete diagnostic work-up. When we reported that this had already been done—each part performed by qualified and competent professionals—they insisted that only their own work-up was acceptable. This could not be scheduled for several months. Their acceptance of Ruby depended on the outcome of the examinations. But even if the findings showed that theirs was a logical setting to serve her, she would have had to wait indefinitely for an opening. Another agency could not work with her until she was several years older.

Another had too long a waiting list. Another was felt to be unsatisfactory from the viewpoint of our team. All were not easily accessible geographically. Some would have necessitated excessively long commutation. Others required her to reside in their facilities. These were some of the factors that moved BOCES * to intervene and provide their services within our community.

We worked with a brother and sister who were both aphasic. To find an appropriate elementary school setting for these children, the parents first did a thorough search and then relocated to a community almost eighty miles away so that the children could attend that school and live at home. These were delightful children, and the devoted parents were able to make the necessary move.

Sometimes inaccessibility results from status needs, or perhaps pomposity would be a better word. I remember explaining something of this nature to one of my own children when she commented that she didn't like a certain physician. She had noticed that he was cold and distant. "He behaves this way because he's not sure of himself," I explained. "After all, he feels that you must be impressed with his knowledge and competence if you are to accept his ability to cor-

---

* Board of Cooperative Education Services, an agency of the New York State Department of Education that cooperates with local school systems in providing occupational training, special education for mentally and physically handicapped children, shared teacher services in remedial areas, testing and counselling services, psychiatric consulting, and data processing services.

rectly diagnose and prescribe for your ailments. I suppose he feels unsure of himself and tries to act important and efficient to impress you."

No one group has a monopoly on pomposity. Sometimes I encounter it in what I call *the calendar game.* I first identified it about twenty years ago when I was conferring with a professional who had been discussing problems he was having in getting his staff to meet with him. Twice during our conversation he received phone calls. Each time he went through an elaborate routine to schedule an appointment. He wasted much time giving gratuitous information about times he was not available, appointments that eliminated certain days, times he had to visit other agencies, and so on, and it took several proposals from each caller before they finally agreed upon an appointment. In effect he was saying, "I'm a busy man; I have many important things to do; I will try to sandwich you in if I can find the time." It was not hard to understand why he had difficulty. His bad example taught me to avoid this sort of snare.

In trying to make good use of the parent-teacher relationship, I have evaluated and reevaluated the ways in which we work together. Some widespread practices have been rejected because they make little sense. Open School Week is one. It might, in some instances, be more appropriately called Closed School Week because the constant waves of spectators, plus the tempting tendency to put on a show, make for distortion and distraction. Instead of this we provide for observation, first at intake for every parent and subsequently by appointment either at a parent's request or at our suggestion. Most of this observation is done through the one-way windows. Observation occurs constantly so neither teachers nor children are self-conscious. It is unobtrusive because it is done from outside the classroom. Sometimes we feel it necessary to have the parent go into the classroom. This, too, is taken in stride—the children are used to other adults visiting with them because college students and teachers from other schools visit in this way.

Conference Day is another rejected practice. I tried it for a while and discovered that it meant scheduling a continuous, tight run of fifteen-minute conferences. These were not really conferences. I soon discovered that to keep to anything like a fifteen-minute schedule, it was necessary to avoid any but superficial concerns. Topics that called for depth of discussion had to be avoided or left for another time. There is little time to allow for the amenities of a normal conversation between human beings who share a common interest. The Conference Line is an even worse variant of tightly scheduled conferences. Parents look at displays and then line up for brief exchanges with the teacher. This ordeal is embarrassing and accomplishes little.

Report cards and other standardized report forms have also been tried and found wanting. I first tried forms that covered a number of facets of childhood learning and development rated on a three point scale: O for outstanding, S for satisfactory, U for unsatisfactory. After using these for two years, I decided they said little and were often unintentionally misleading. Then I developed a form intended to yield a comprehensive narrative report. It was divided into four sections: physical development, social and emotional development, program participation, and general appraisal. Under each heading were a series of suggestions on what could be covered. For example, those for program participation were: special interests, likes and dislikes, work habits, approach to and use of materials and equipment, attitude toward program, participation in group planning, reaction to routines such as dressing and undressing, rest, snack, cleanup, and loading and unloading buses. Paradoxically this report impressed many parents, but I found it a failure. The teachers had difficulty using it, and it gave parents an inadequate picture of their child.

In evaluating these and other common practices, I discovered that many had become formalized and standardized but did little to help the child or to give parents information and assistance that would meaningfully include him in the teaching–learning process. There had to be better ways of working with parents. Instead of looking for one particular method, I gradually evolved a variety of approaches that allowed us to work with parents on an individualized basis, just as we work with their children.

Discarding the standardized procedures frees all of us from wasting the time they require. At the same time, it clearly means that we must make sure that appropriate provision is made for each parent. Taking my cue from the *calendar game* experience, I let it be known that I am readily accessible. This leaves me open for exploitation by those who have no regard for another's commitments or responsibilities, but experience has taught me how to be accessible and yet avoid exploitation. I am easily reached by phone, and if I am not in the middle of something, I'm usually willing to enter into discussion immediately. If I can deal with a problem or question in this way, I do so. If I am lacking information, I arrange to get it and call back. If it is something that requires more thought or perhaps further observations of a child, I make a conference date, allowing enough time for study or observation.

I call parents often, sometimes simply to ask questions or give information about a child, and sometimes to arrange for a conference.

Some parents request a written report. We oblige by making one in narrative form.

Each parent comes in person for an intake interview, and that session is directed at giving him orientation and understanding of what we are trying to do and what he might expect as his child goes through this experience.

We have a parents' library that allows them to borrow books that might further their understanding. We also have pamphlets and circular announcements that give them information about local places and events that interest children. We also send them book offerings that enable them to build their children's libraries. We also send them notices of such events as the Free Amblyopia Examination sponsored by the Womens Auxiliary of the County Medical Society. This year we worked with the Auxiliary to try a pilot, free hearing test for all the children at the school. (It is hoped that this experience will enable the Auxiliary to provide this test to all the children in the community.)

Twice a year we have parents' meetings to give

parents an overview of what we are doing. This enables them to see beyond the evasions they get when they ask their youngsters:

"Where did you go?"

"Out."

"What did you do?"

"Nothing."

More About
ooooooooooooooooooooooooooooo Families

Before my son began kindergarten, his teacher came to visit our home to become acquainted. She chatted with him and had a cup of coffee with Mrs. Gilbert. Everyone of her prospective pupils and their parents had a similar visit. This was done at the teacher's initiative on her own time. When Mrs. Gilbert told me about it, I smiled and commented, "I wish every elementary classroom could begin with the teacher getting a chance to know something about each child, his family, and their life style." Other teachers I have met share this feeling.

At the opposite pole are teachers whose "expertise" is so instantaneous they need only glimpse at a classroom to tell you all about the children in it. One such judgement came from a teacher who was visiting my school, "You're lucky. You school serves the well-to-do, middle-class kids whose mommies and daddies are education-minded."

As gently as I could, I took an opposing viewpoint, "By putting all the kids into one lump sum category, you don't see them as they really are."

To prove my point, I invited her to accompany me on one of our bus routes. The novelty of the offer appealed to her. As we rode past their houses, I described the children's families, singling out information that helped me see each child as a distinct individual. Our area is quite rural. The size of the plot and house style seem obvious clues to the likely income of the occupants. X-ray eyes would reveal only the bare essentials of furniture in many homes or others with museum like "living rooms," off-limits to children. Such inside information still leaves big gaps in understanding.

Every stop along our route gave me an opportunity to give information about a child and his family that needs to be known by a teacher. I particularly remember our conversations at five stops. At two of these, elderly women put the children on the bus. The first time this happened the teacher observed, "She's pretty old to be working as a housekeeper." I replied, "That's Jane's grandmother. Theirs is a three-generation household. The retired grandparents are the homemakers, and both parents work full-time."

"Another grandmother?" she asked when the next elderly lady appeared. Her putting this in question form made me feel we were making progress. "Yes," I answered, "but not of this family. She is employed here as homemaker for a widower and his young children. Luckily she gives these children the kind of loving care they really need."

Another Tweedle Dum and Tweedle Dee situation proved to have entirely different particulars. In each instance the child was put on the bus by an attractive, well dressed young mother, who took off in her convertible when our bus left. At the first of these stops the teacher looked at the home, the convertible, and the well groomed mother and said, "They must be loaded." "I wouldn't know," I answered. "The mother spends her afternoons selling cosmetics in people's homes. The father moonlights on a second job till ten p.m. every night."

Her seeming twin also proved to be a puzzler. When we reached the second mother at her convertible, I commented, "This girl's father told me that she was being sent to school because he wanted his wife to have her afternoons free."

The fifth memorable exchange took place when a child came out from an old mansion. The teacher was surprised at the mother's appearance because she was wearing just a housedress. "That's a multiple family residence," I explained. "The family lives in very modest circumstances. John is their foster child whose nursery school tuition is provided by the family service agency."

At the end of our ride I added, "I set up the bus routes every year, and each one has had an equally diverse group of people." My attempt to drive that teacher towards understanding was a spur of the moment act.

I recently visited the Mechanicstown School, where this idea was refined into a staff training procedure. This school is located in a low income area of the Middletown (New York) school district. Of a total of 380 students, 75 are on a free breakfast and lunch program. A balance in the student body has been achieved by busing in children from middle- and upper-middle income areas. The school's principal, William Carter, brings much skill to this setting. His "traveling staff meeting" is among the ideas that have built a we feeling in the school. This meeting is held on a bus that follows the usual morning route so the teachers can see and talk about the neighborhoods of their students.

When I asked Mr. Carter what he thought resulted from the conference, he said, "A much better student-teacher relationship can be had when the teacher is aware of a child's home situation. Next year we hope to have one parent from each neighborhood on the bus to tell us something about that area."

"You should have seen the teachers' faces when we passed the Joad house," he continued. "Tim Joad attends our school, and there are three younger children at home. Their home is a condemned shack. It has no utilities. To get water, someone in the family goes to a neighbor a half-mile down the road. The yard near the house has a gaping hole where the father dug in an unsuccessful attempt to hook into the water main. Before that bus ride Tim was constantly in trouble. The teachers were always complaining about him or punishing him. After seeing his home, everybody was on his side. Instead of constantly watching to keep him in check, they found ways to give him help and praise."

Another result of this bus ride was an experimental open classroom. Seeing the children's homes and neighborhoods made the staff aware that the learning experiences at school had to be better adapted to the needs of the children. Some curriculum materials were totally irrelevant to the life styles of Tim and many others. Through the open classroom the teachers hoped to provide curriculum options that could build upon the life experiences of these children.

In seeking new roads to understanding, I do not overlook the ones that come through my own front door. Parents who do their own transporting are usually the ones we get to know best. They, in turn, have many chances to observe classes, meet their children's friends and other parents, and talk with the teachers.

At P.S. 39, an inner-city school, this approach has been implemented by using a classroom as a parents' meeting room. This school is located in the Hunts Point area of the Bronx. There is no transporting. The school serves the near neighborhood, whose ethnic description is sixty-five percent Puerto Rican, thirty percent black, and five percent other Hispanic Americans. Here is a statistic that could serve as an index of the poverty in the community: from a total of 1,500 students, 1,200 are in the free lunch program.

The parents' room began in 1966 as a feature of the Head Start program. Its use has been carried forward by the Parents' Association. Lawrence Hirsch, the principal, says, "I enter that room as a guest of the parents, and I see many worthwhile things come from it."

It is simply furnished with tables and chairs. The school contributed an old sewing machine that had once been used for training retarded children. Funds from the Parents' Association purchased an additional sewing machine, a file of clothes patterns, and a coffee urn. The parents come to talk and sew and drink coffee.

Some teachers worried about this room at first. Their

fears were somewhat realized. The room did produce headaches, but in many instances the Parents' Association served as an ombudsman in helping solve problems that arose in school. The parents set up a series of programs covering welfare rights, rent counselling, mental health, planned parenthood, and a workshop on how to evaluate a school. One of the mothers even conducted a thrice weekly exercise course. This was announced by a sign on the door stating "For Women Only—No Men Allowed." When Mr. Hirsch asked why men were barred, he was told, "When we feel in shape to show ourselves in leotards, we'll invite you in."

chapter 6 ∘∘∘∘∘∘∘∘∘∘∘∘∘∘∘∘∘∘∘∘∘∘∘

Learning About Themselves ∘∘∘∘∘∘∘∘∘∘∘∘∘∘∘∘ and Others

The ability to learn is an attribute of all human beings. Each child comes to school with this ability, but many do not fulfill their potential. There are always reasons for underachievement. Some of these weaknesses may be overcome with the help of the teacher, who sees the child as a whole person and reaches him through understanding. This chapter describes what happens as children *learn about themselves and others,* one of the prime objectives of my school.

○ STEVIE, *The Grabber*
"Tommy must learn how to share. I know he will learn it here."

My response to Tommy's mother took the form of a story about Stevie the Grabber. That nickname was bestowed by one of his victims who had more than her fill of him one particular day. On the way home she sat next to me and gave vent to her feelings:

"That Stevie thinks he owns everything! Whatever he wants, he takes! I'm going to call him Stevie the Grabber."

Her description was accurate. Despite the staff's attempts to discard it, the nickname persisted for some time because it was apt.

Stevie had good reason to act this way. He came to us an uncrowned king. He was his family's only boy. He had two sisters, ten and twelve years older than he, and two doting parents. At home whatever Stevie wanted, Stevie got. He came to school expecting more of the same. To some extent he succeeded in carrying this off, but resistance and countermeasures from his would-be-victims inevitably came into play. Stevie gradually mended his ways. Before much time had passed, he discovered that he could talk his classmates out of almost anything.

"It wouldn't have surprised me to see one of them smilingly give Stevie his eye teeth," I recalled to Tommy's mother. "You see he remained as acquisitive as he was when he first came, but he learned to modify his behavior to what was more acceptable to his classmates. I'm not sure whether you had this sort of thing in mind when you proposed that we teach children how to share. Stevie's ideas on sharing were much the same as before, but his behavior towards his classmates changed to more reasonably provide for their rights and their feelings."

As I was telling this story to several parents recently I added, "You see, we do not try to make a child over, we simply seek to help him learn how to reasonably moderate his behavior."

One of the mothers commented, "I'm not sure you

would want to make him over even if you could. Who knows but that Stevie's acquisitiveness may eventually develop into a quality that benefits him and others as well."

There are many acceptable solutions to the problems that occur in human relationships. Too often adults expect model behavior from children. They are expected to learn virtues that do not abound in our society. Individuals who grow to adulthood with only the fine graces as their personality components are apt to have highly fragile egos. These are not people who can withstand stress. The narrow limits of their personalities do not equip them to function effectively in a wide range of circumstances.

Had we intended to make over Stevie, it would have been an exercise in futility. This is not our function. Trying to do this would be like planting a sunflower seed and expecting to grow a rose. Stevie and every other child comes to school as an individual. It is our desire and function to help them develop their individual capacities.

○ FRANKIE, *The Pincher*

Frankie pinched. He was good at it. Mrs. Gilbert, his teacher, reaches children well. They open up easily to her because she is an excellent listener. I watched through the observation window. Frankie caused furrows in his teacher's brow. His skillful pinches found tender targets on his playmates.

In less than one month three parents called. Each of their conversations began, "Is there a boy named Frankie in so and so's class?"

"Yes."

"Do you know that Frankie pinches?"

"Yes."

From this point on the discussion took diverse routes. The substance, however, was similar. Reassurance was given that we were aware of Frankie's pinching and that it was certainly annoying, but little more than that. We regarded the pinching and all that followed as an opportunity far more than a problem. In situations where parents or teachers are involved, we can be instrumental in seeing that worth-while learning occurs. Similar situations arise in random play, but the learning there is as likely to be bad as to be good. The experience of Frankie and his classmates will be more fully understood if one realizes that parents who did not call were also involved.

There is little doubt that Frankie tried pinching most of his classmates. One or two may have screamed loudly and thus given him the message that they would attract too much attention from the teachers. Others may have managed to dissuade him by telling him off effectively. The apparent strength and physical prowess of some may have suggested that he could choose safer victims. Certainly some of them must have complained to their parents and experienced a variety of reactions. The nonchalance of one parent may have impressed his child that the pinching wasn't really a big thing. Another may have given the old eye-for-eye, tooth-for-tooth instructions and sent his child back to school trained and practiced in pinching back. Probably some parents were too busy to pay attention and thus made their children aware that they would have to solve the problem themselves.

Each of the pinches and the reactions was part of the

learning process for Frankie and his classmates. All involved learned from these experiences. No one solution enabled Frankie to see the light. Each, however, helped.

Mrs. Gilbert and her aide, Mrs. Lomnitz, were aware of more than the pinching. In observing and conferring about Frankie we decided that he wasn't used to playing with other children. Mrs. Lomnitz also was his bus driver. She knows the community well, having lived here since its early stages of growth and development. She is quick at picking up clues that help us better understand a child. She discovered that Frankie had no playmates near his home. His mother confirmed this. We gave her the names of several of his classmates, suggesting that they visit in each others' homes to extend and strengthen relationships begun at school.

We believed that Frankie's pinching was an act of reaching out to playmates of his own age as if saying, "I have so little chance to play with someone my own age. Please notice me!" Time and again we have observed that a child who has few playmates living near him reaches out in some physical way, as if expressing his yearning for companionship.

One of the three mothers whom I phoned explained to her son Jimmy, a classmate of Frankie's, that what Frankie needed most was a friend. I had made this point to her during our conversation. As Jimmy boarded the school bus the next day, he greeted the driver with the announcement, "I'm going to be Frankie's friend."

Pinching was noted as one small piece of the puzzle of Frankie, and effort was directed at finding out more about him that would enable us to understand why he pinched. Each staff member involved with him observed and shared his observations with the others. His mother was consulted and advised. His interaction with other children was treated with understanding, and the staff concentrated more on helping them enjoy each other than in refereeing their disagreements. Other parents concerned about the pinching called and were given information to make them more aware of how they could help. Finally Jimmy enunciated the understanding we were all seeking. We were, at this point, pleased with Jimmy's announcement, but had no expectations of him carrying out his noble resolve. Jimmy and Frankie seemed not likely to become friends. Jimmy was a brain; Frankie was always in motion and seemed to be unaware of how to relate through words. To our utter amazement they did become friends. Jimmy became to Frankie what an ice cream cone is to a sweet tooth. Jimmy equally enjoyed and benefitted from the relationship. Frankie stopped pinching. He soon made other friends. His play interests widened, and his learning through his school experiences really progressed well.

○ CLARA, *The Hair Puller*

"Pinch him back!" or its rough equivalent, "If he hits you, hit him back!" is advice given too often. It sometimes solves the problem, but it often does not. A child who lacks sufficient brawn to come out well in a brawl is likely to invite more grief if he tries hitting back. A child who is strong doesn't greatly benefit either because he learns to rely on his brawn rather than his brain.

"When she pulls your hair, you pull hers!" was the

advice Mrs. Kane gave her daughter Betty. She told me about this when she informed me that Clara always pulled Betty's hair.

"That may not have been the best idea," I replied. "Clara is one of the youngest in the class. Both of her parents work. When she began nursery school, she also began with a new sitter. She has no children living near her. When the class is sitting for such activities as story-time, she often sits behind one of the girls and strokes her hair. Sometimes the stroking is enjoyed or tolerated, but Betty pushes Clara's hands away and then gets her hair pulled. Several times Clara cried after these exchanges. Clara badly wants and needs Betty's friendship."

Mrs. Kane understood and said she would help Betty find other ways to handle the hair pulling.

○ IRA, *The Irascible*
Sometimes a child misuses an adult until the adult alters his role or relationship to overcome the way he is being used.

"At last he's overcoming his timidity and asserting himself! He probably never will be a lion tamer, but when he began here, he was a Casper Milquetoast. He was bullied and cowed by the others. When someone wanted his toy, he surrendered it without a murmur. Now he says, 'I got this first! It's *mine*' and he hangs on to it."

That was part of the description of Ira Drew's progress that I gave to his mother during a conference in February.

"Is he becoming a bully?" she asked.

"No," I reassured her. "He is learning to stand up for his rights, and this is an important piece of learning for him."

"I'm happy to hear this," she replied, "but he has become a problem at home. He has a terrible temper. Several times he has come off the school bus, viciously kicked a friend who was waiting for him, and then ran away before any of us knew what was happening."

We had seen no such behavior at school, and I said we would have told her about it if we had. I reemphasized our satisfaction with the progress he had made, and the discussion turned to other concerns.

About two weeks later Ira became irascible at school. Flareups of temper and vicious hittings occurred again and again. After it happened a number of times, his teacher noticed that it always occurred when she was nearby. Mrs. Ghosio, his teacher, is used to children's rough and tumble ways. She grew up on a farm, climbs trees, and loves animals, even when they take hard nips at her fingers. She had noticed Ira's early timidity and had commented that he was "afraid of too many things." Now his behavior was changing. More and more she was finding it necessary to intercede to prevent brawls between him and his classmates. When we talked about it, she postulated that he seemed to be using her. He hit out, knowing she would not let a fight develop.

We decided to try a drastic cure. She began by explaining to Ira that she wanted him to stop and that if he did not, she would allow the others to hit back. For a while this worked, but then Ira's temper outbursts and hitting started again. Again he was warned, but he didn't believe the warning would be carried out. He found that he could get his licks in and then Mrs. Ghosio would intervene. She waited until he picked on a child who could stand up to him, and she then told the child that he could hit back and could do it again if Ira hit him. A brawl ensued. Ira punched and was punched back. He kicked and was kicked back. They wrestled to the floor and turned over and under as each tried to gain a decisive advantage. They were equally matched, and the fight was soon stopped, but not before Mrs. Ghosio made sure that Ira understood that he could no longer use her to bully others. Ira's understanding came, of course, after a few more tests. In the meantime we shared our observations and experiences with Mrs. Drew, and she agreed to follow a similar course of action. Before long his temper flare-ups stopped.

The teacher needs to see that she is a part of the interaction that takes place in her class. The roles she assumes have impact on the child's experiences. The way Ira used his teacher (and his mother) illustrates this. There are many other ways that children use the benign presence of an adult.

○ JENNIE, *The Crier*

Jennie cried. She cried about many things. Her cries and sobs wracked her body. It was pitiful to behold. Mrs. Dean, her teacher, quickly embraced and reassured her and tried to help her overcome her fears. It soon became obvious that Jennie had many many sources of fear. She gave the appearance of being fragile, but if one looked carefully, he saw that she was tall, well built, and well coordinated. This made it particularly ridiculous when she ran terrified to Mrs. Dean because Herbie, a little mischief about two heads shorter than Jennie, threatened her by saying "I'm gonna kill you!"

Jennie couldn't have known what she did for Herbie's ego. When he discovered he could terrorize her by this threat, he was delighted. He might not have been so proud of himself if he had realized she was too easy a mark. Jennie cried about almost anything. She cried when teased, she cried when scolded, she cried when she wanted something, she cried when somebody refused to play with her.

Mrs. Dean and Mrs. Crandall, her teacher's aide, seemed a perfect pair of patsies for Jennie. Each has five children of her own—plus two grandchildren for Mrs. Dean. When Mrs. Dean began working at school, she freely acknowledged that she was not highly organized. I discovered that she had other qualities that more than compensated. Her anecdotal records are excellent. As I read them, I realized she not only sees each child but that she perceives even more. Mrs. Crandall is equally perceptive. They make a wonderful team. More than a few times they have demonstrated special compassion for a child in need.

In Jennie's case their compassion needed some tempering. Jennie's mode of solving problems was to cry, heartrendingly, until nearby adults solved her problem. Once we recognized the pattern, we started trying to teach her to solve her own problems. This was not easy. We slowly realized that her mother would have to be included in our efforts. I phoned her.

"Mrs. Warren," I began, "Jennie cries too much. She cries about everything under the sun. When children tease her, she cries and expects us to get them to stop. We've tried getting her to cope herself. We've as much as told her what to say. We make it clear that we won't let anyone harm her but that she needs to learn how to speak up for herself. I suspect that you must be solving too many of her problems for her and she expects us to do the same."

Mrs. Warren sighed. She knew exactly what I was talking about. This was one of her reasons for sending Jennie to nursery school.

"You must learn to let her solve her problems herself."

"I know she needs to learn how to speak out. Mr. Warren never raises his voice. He has great responsibility in his business and he has much aggravation. In fact, he is under so much pressure that he has an ulcer."

"Ulcers are exactly what we're talking about," I interjected. "Until and unless Jennie learns to relate to others with the normal kinds of emotions, including anger and shouting or snapping back at those who tease her, she will repress her feelings or become a perpetual whiner. Repressed feelings trigger ailments like ulcers or other conditions that have psychosomatic components."

We went on to explain that feelings are intended to be expressed and Jennie needed to learn how to act out anger or disapproval without crying for mommy or a convenient substitute.

The conversation ended with Mrs. Warren's agreement to do her best to let Jennie learn how to solve

Learning About Themselves and Others ❧ 69

her own problems. Slowly, but gradually, our combined efforts enabled Jennie to stand up for herself instead of constantly crying for help.

○ BARRY, *The Angelic*

Some parents become intrusive the moment they set foot in school. Mrs. Grace did not. She called beforehand, came at the appointed time, asked meaningful questions, and observed carefully. After five such visits I wondered what she was looking for. Her child was not in school; she came to determine if the school was appropriate. My patience would usually have worn thin by this time, but there was something about Mrs. Grace, my intuition told me, that merited my patience. The five observation sessions were spaced within two months. At the end of the fifth, as at the end of each of the others, she said goodbye and left looking as though she was preoccupied with making careful evaluation of what she had seen. Several weeks passed, and then she called for an intake appointment.

By the time she arrived for the interview, I was filled with curiosity about her five visits. This time she came with her three-year-old son, Barry, who quietly joined a class at play. The discussion began. Before I could raise a question, Mrs. Grace said, "I am a widow. Barry has been left with sitters since he was an infant, because I go to work."

At that moment I was grateful for the intuition that counselled patience. I explained the workings of this school to Mrs. Grace, and as we spoke, she told me more about Barry and herself.

Barry began school the following September. He took part in all activities. He played well with his classmates. He conformed to all routines. He created no problems. It would seem that we should have been perfectly content—but we weren't. Something just wasn't right—Barry was too good. Whatever was asked of him, he tried to do; but as he did it, it seemed that he was conforming with no reluctance or resistance, but also without great interest or desire. His work lacked distinctive characteristics; it was stilted and barren. He used paint as though it were rationed. His collages were inevitably three small pieces of paper neatly glued to a large piece of paper. He answered questions but never spoke out of turn. He never allowed his play to involve him in conflict. He never asserted his desires nor made demands of others.

We could almost see a sword of Damocles perpetually suspended over his head. We could imagine Mrs. Grace leaving him with baby sitters, cautioning that he behave or else the delicate balance of their situation would be disturbed. Their dependence on the good graces of the sitters was shaping Barry's personality as the ancient custom of binding feet stunted the healthy growth of the feet of Chinese girls. We wanted Barry to realize that he could be himself without fear, that he was free to play, to try out all kinds of behavior, to assert, to explore, to discover, to learn, to enjoy, to test, to fail—and that we would be accepting of him—bad, good, happy or angry.

I told Mrs. Grace of our concern, and she agreed to help, even though she wasn't sure of what we were hoping to do. To Barry we made it clear by our attitudes and actions that we accepted children as they were. He could see how other children behaved, and when appropriate incidents occurred, we would explain for anyone to hear (especially Barry) that, "It is no calamity to do something wrong. That is one way we learn. Next time we can try to do it right. Sometimes we do things wrong many times before we learn how to do them right, but we need chances to try over and over again, if we expect to learn." Saying this and other things in a similar vein was our means of telling Barry how we felt and giving him the go-ahead sign that at school he was free to be himself. Demonstrating this to him in our interaction with his classmates and with him (when he gave us a chance) was another part of the experience. Patiently allowing time for the experiences to take effect was a third essential.

At the end of November, after almost three months, two dramatic signs of change occurred. First, we noticed Barry's paintings had become alive. Instead of the three or four ceremonial strokes, there were people, and clouds, and the sun, and grass, and multi-colored raindrops. The change from the old mode of painting to the new was sudden. Just as suddenly Barry became a chatterbox, and much like the unfolding of a flower bud, the personality of the real Barry opened out.

He talked out of turn and had to be told to be quiet. He tested limits and had to have them explained and enforced. Although these new modes of behavior placed some strains on teachers and playmates, we welcomed them as signs that Barry knew he was free to be himself.

The need to realize fulfillment is universal.

To avoid misinterpretation of the narrative about Barry, his change from restraint to assertiveness should not be construed as the goal. In his instance the restraint was unnatural. We have no desire to change lambs into lions. Each child is seen as a distinct individual and valued as he is. Restraint, shyness, quietness, and timidity are considered good qualities, and so are boldness, gregariousness, and assertiveness.

○ HEIDI, The Sensitive
Many times parents have shown much concern about a sensitive child. In more than a few instances these children have shown accompanying qualities that more than balanced the sensitivity.

Heidi was physically unattractive, and clumsy as well, but her homely face became alive with animation and interest as soon as she got together with her friends. And she had many friends. Other children sought her out because of her wonderful responsiveness to them, to their plans, to their experiences, and the delightful way she related her own experiences to theirs.

Her mother was confused by the contradiction between the complaints Heidi brought home and her eagerness to return to school the next day: "She comes home with all her problems! 'Betty always makes me play dress-up. She always is the mommy. I have to be the baby.' 'Frankie pinches me. He's not nice.' 'Audrey took my doll, but she wouldn't let me play with her Show and Tell.' 'I don't want to be in that class. Herbie always teases me.' But when the school bus comes the next day, she runs to it eagerly, with a big smile."

Heidi, like many others, found mother her perfect sounding board. She reserved her special hurt feelings for their times together, and played out her strains and plaints to her mother's sympathetic vibrations.

The same sensitivity that gave her so much awareness of others' feelings caused her fair grief when she experienced rebuffs. As the old refrain goes, "You can't have one without the other." When we looked through our anecdotals, we found them filled with incidents that showed clearly how she sensed and responded to her friends' needs. Giving up her doll despite Audrey's selfish response was one example. Her subsequent complaint to her mother showed another facet of her feelings. Those of us on the school staff who worked closest with her were unanimous in our appreciation of her fine qualities and in our enjoyment of her. So was her mother. The problem of what to do about the hurts she experienced was not overlooked.

We made sure to let her know the delight she gave her friends and us by her many thoughtful acts. When Heidi did a good deed and was, in turn, done wrong, Mrs. Dean would say, "Well, you can't win them all!" and the feeling tone of her remark made it clear that she empathized with Heidi and was gently helping her over a letdown and hurt. Mrs. Dean has a wry humor that is at the same time affectionate and disarming, and effectively lets a child know she's with you. Or Mrs. Crandall, in her gentle way, would directly thank Heidi for the help she gave another child. By these and other ways we made it clear that we found her special because of her wonderful sensitivity. I believe that helped her gain more feeling of security and the ability to handle the accompanying hurts.

○ ERNEST, *The Baby Doll*
Failures have as much significance in the teaching-learning process as do successes. Ernest was one of our failures. He was quite immature. Several interactions observed between Ernest and his parents and older sib-

lings made us believe that they regarded him as a real live baby doll. They dressed him like a baby doll. They addressed him as a baby doll. His toys were those of a baby. He was lifted onto and off the bus and often carried from his house to the bus. When I spoke to the parents, "the baby" was their designation for him. His dress, his speech, his mannerisms, and his modes of relating to peers and adults were those of a younger child. His physical appearance was normal. He was handsome, well built, and well coordinated. When he wasn't working at acting out the baby, he showed much evidence of good intelligence.

I shared the staff's observations with his parents. We felt that in treating him like a baby, they were perpetuating his infancy and denying him appropriate challenges, growth and developmental opportunities. He lapped up their lavish affection and wanted more of the same from his teachers and classmates. This could have continued for some time. I felt it incumbent upon me to spell out its implications, especially that his prime learning time was being usurped by the needs of the family to have a baby doll. If this continued, in two years time he would be far behind in his development. My phrasing was direct but tactful.

The parents' reaction was indignation.

Ernest's progress was too slow. Our ability to affect it appeared to depend on cooperative efforts of the parents. Silence could have maintained the *status quo,* but that would have meant ignoring the child's real needs and just putting him through the time and motions of going to school. A second conference resulted in the parents withdrawing the child. This represents failure up to that point, but the parents may find themselves pursued by a nagging doubt that may cause them to reexamine their relationship with Ernest. If, however, their relationship does not change, the problem will intensify, and they are likely to have some aspect of it called to their attention. Even in our seeming failure we laid the groundwork for the next time the problem confronts the parents. This reassures us that there is good reason for us to function honestly and openly with parents.

○ DAVID and LISA, *The Inseparables*

The need to be needed is in each of us. To fulfill this need well requires intelligence, judgment, patience, persistence, and especially the ability to take a long view of a helping relationship. Oftentimes what seems to be helpful is the opposite. Every year a number of parents request that their children be placed in the same class as their close friends. If I sense the request to be more than casual, I push the discussion on it. Often I discover that a parent is an unwitting partner in creating a dependency relationship.

David and Lisa were a classic example. Lisa led David by the nose, and he loved it and so did she. He followed her around the classroom doing whatever she wished. Sometimes she gave him opportunity to choose the play, but she inevitably made the final decision. She made other friends, especially with girls, and these relationships were far more satisfactory in terms of give-and-take. David had only Lisa. He would play with nobody else as long as she was in class. When she was absent, he sometimes found another playmate, but more usually he moped away. Lisa was not benefitting from her role as dominator. She consumed his affection and demanded more. He dutifully bent to her will, and she became increasingly wilful in her demands.

We were having no success in moving him into other relationships. If their records had shown them to live on the same block, we would immediately have been aware that this was a carry-over of a neighborhood relationship. However, they lived on different streets, so I assumed their relationship began at school. Only when I called David's mother did we learn that they lived near enough to be able to walk to each others homes and that at home, too, David was Lisa's devoted slave.

Mrs. MacLean, David's mother, wasn't sure how she felt about this relationship. "David is very sensitive, and the boys in the neighborhood bully him." Listening carefully, I could discern that Mrs. MacLean also was sensitive. She made it clear that when David ran home crying from an encounter with one of the boys, she was torn with compassion for his hurts.

"You know," I explained, "almost everyone of us feels as you do. When my child is hurt, I feel his pain. It seems to me that you and I and many other parents are like the twin Corsican brothers in Dumas' tale who by an accident of birth share one sense of feeling, so that when the one is stabbed, the other suffers. This degree of sensitivity that makes many of us feel our children's trials and tribulations is all to the good—*if* we remember that we are parents and that by virtue of our age and experience we have lived through childhood relationships and can therefore effectively help our children." Again I reminded her that one of the best things any parent or teacher can do for a child is teach him to help himself.

Mrs. MacLean's problem was not resolved in only one conference. Two of these were face-to-face, and the others were phone calls covering specific items of concern. She gradually came to see David's relationship with Lisa for what it was and also became increasingly aware that David was developing almost no ability to handle the usual kinds of interaction with other boys. David's father became a participant in this process. He was upset because David was such a sissy. Mrs. MacLean, in turn, was upset because her husband showed so little patience with David. "Why, when I was his age . . ." began Mr. MacLean, and he then proceeded to unravel what sounded like several real life episodes from Tom Sawyer and Huckleberry Finn. I, too, drew upon some childhood experiences, but in mine, in addition to my acts of bravery, I also included such examples of sheer cowardice as when I made a very hurried trip home from school one day when a classmate, big Molly Malone, threatened to seek me out and pin my ears back. This and other exchanges relaxed Mr. MacLean to the point of his confessing a few human weaknesses. Then we were able to get to the heart of the situation.

"I often wish," said I, "that each of us could have some of the first works that we made when we were young children. We would then be far more likely to appreciate our children's early efforts." To drive home my point I took the MacLeans through a classroom and showed them the works of the children and explained them in terms of what we know about early child development and the learning needs of the young child. By the end of the conference Mr. MacLean showed more appreciation of his importance in David's development. I emphasized that the relationship of father and son was a key factor.

Subsequent developments in their relationship proved that our conference had been worthwhile. One item worth mentioning was a project that started within a week of the conference—David and his father went shopping together for a set of tools, and then they built a workbench for David which he used well for some time thereafter.

Resolution of the relationship between David and Lisa necessitated putting Lisa in a different class. This made it necessary for David to find new friends. He wasn't happy at first, but soon proved fully capable, and his later development was so delightful that it served to emphasize how ridiculous the dependency relationship had been—how potentially destructive it could have been if it had been allowed to persist.

No one factor was totally responsible for David's effective adjustment. The separation from Lisa was certainly catalytic. It is easy to see that as long as they were in the same class, we gave the green light to their ongoing relationship. Once they were separated, David had to function alone. And he soon discovered he was fully capable of doing so.

The separation of David and Lisa appears much simpler viewed by hindsight than it did at the time we had to effectuate it. David and Lisa and their parents were ready with various defenses when the time came to put them in different classes. We acted resolutely with calm assurance and proved that the fetish of their dependency was sheer bunkum.

○ CONSTANCE, *The Invisible*

Because he causes nobody difficulty, an undemanding child can conceal real problems.

Constance was the quietest of children—so quiet that one had to look twice to be sure she was there. She demanded nothing of anyone, neither teachers nor the other children. She could easily have been lost within the classroom, and it seemed as if that was what she wanted. She played with others, but more as a tag-alonger than an active participant. The other children accepted her but did not seek her out. The art works she produced were done *pro forma*. Even one accustomed to seeing children's first works could find no particular significance in what she made. When the time of day came for each child to claim his works, she took only what others identified for her and then left it in school or on the bus. Her complete passivity was a mystery. She had no distinctive physical characteristic nor mannerism. Her short, unkempt hair was a possible exception. In addition to being short and poorly combed, it looked as though she had given herself a haircut.

During our first conference her mother had expressed concern that Constance was overly dependent on two older brothers and a sister, ages five, seven, and eight (Constance was then three). She seemed unable to move out of their shadows. Each of them had some outstanding quality, but Constance had none.

That haircut we thought she had given herself proved to be our first gleaning of understanding. Mrs. Dean observed that it seemed never to grow in properly and asked whether she kept cutting it or whether she had some defect in hair growth. To our surprise we learned that she pulled her hair out by the fistful.

The second significant clue came when Constance stayed for four days with an elderly maiden aunt. Aunt Margaret was the one person Constance obviously enjoyed, and it was equally apparent that Aunt Margaret looked upon Constance as someone special. During the days she was staying with Aunt Margaret, Constance painted and made collages and anxiously claimed them to take home to the doting aunt.

We began to realize that Constance's greatest need was "a place in the sun." We called and spoke with her mother to tell her what we observed. We explained that Constance's most apparent need was more attention. At school we tried giving her extra measures of tender loving care and found her increasingly responsive. We felt she needed opportunities at home to get out from under her siblings' shadows. She needed extra love, attention, and approval whenever reasonable opportunities presented themselves, and opportunities might have to be created, if not enough presented themselves naturally. Her mother seemed to grow relieved as this conversation proceeded. She agreed that she had some awareness that Constance needed more affection and attention, but didn't quite "know how to reach her."

"She is a very young child," I replied, "and if you are puzzled over how to reach her, you can be sure she is much more puzzled about how to reach you and the rest of the family." I went on to suggest that the mother talk this through with the father and then with the brothers and sister, and that they try by whatever means they could to reach out to her and give her a chance to emerge as an individual.

Precisely what ways they found I do not know. Whether they were ingenious or clumsily contrived we did not discover. But gradually Constance began to change. By the year's end she was not vivacious, loquacious, and the epitome of all talents. However, she did begin to function, to make things, to make demands on others, and to express her feelings. Her hair grew in completely.

It is almost strange to think that "pulling one's hair out" is an idiom used to describe frustration. Constance was acting out that idiom, and if we hadn't watched her closely, she might have disappeared into the woodwork, clutching fistfulls of hair.

Many Constances are lost in many classrooms. To really see her, we had to make conscious efforts and then keep observing, recording, and evaluating.

○ BETH, *The Helper,* and KAREN, *The Helped*
Children can sometimes help other children more effectively than adults can. This was touchingly shown in the way Beth helped Karen emerge from her shell. The death of her mother and the subsequent move to a new community were almost too much for Karen to handle. We took her into school because we knew of these circumstances. When I spoke to her father, he was worried because she was so sad and withdrew from contacts with everyone other than him and her older sister. She tried to hide when people visited at her home. Once she hid under her bed, another time in her closet.

Her sadness was apparent from the moment she

began school. Beth seemed to sense Karen needed a friend, and she went to her immediately. Karen enjoyed Beth. They played well together. Beth's interest in school and in her classmates was infectious. In addition to her ability to relate well, she had a lively imagination. At the time her friendship with Karen began, Beth decided that she was a sorceress and with some incantations she managed to cause it to rain. We joined in the fun of this fantasy, and when that rain stretched into the second week, Beth started looking for a place to hide as we kidded her about it.

They began to visit at each other's home. Karen's father noticed the change and so did her grandmother, who, in addition to caring for her own household, was helping care for the grandchildren. To all of us it was apparent that Karen was doing well. Her relationship with Beth had been a key factor. This was all the more remarkable because at almost the same time Karen lost her mother, Beth's father had died.

○ LIONEL, *The Silent*
Not always are children so benign in their helping ways. Lionel, age three, quickly discovered differences between his classmates and adults. He had been a sickly infant, and his parents had become overly solicitous. His shy smile of entreaty evoked their concern and action. A grimace was even more effective. He seldom spoke. His parents had learned to premeditate his wants, and he seemed to enjoy this pattern of relationship. He clearly intended to carry it over into his school relationships.

His classmates, however, ignored his gestures. They knew he could talk and made no special concessions to him. He soon realized he had to speak up, and before long his shouts could be heard along with his playmates as they gleefully played games of chase. In the meantime, Mrs. Rosenthal and Mrs. Lawrence, who are usually sensitive and responsive, deliberately avoided responding to Lionel's gestures. This, added to the leverage provided by his chatterings with his chums, convinced him that speech was appropriate

currency in school. When we passed this information on to his parents, they were able to effectuate the same change in their relationship with Lionel.

The more one sees how well children help each other, the more one appreciates its importance. It also makes you wonder why the prevailing style in the classroom is horizontal grouping with minimal freedom of interaction. This approach, in effect, shuts out an important ingredient in the teaching–learning process.

○ SARA, *The Giver*

Children who have no siblings benefit much from the interaction they experience in our classrooms. The constant give-and-take provides them with many opportunities to experience a wide range of relationships that compares reasonably well with sibling relationships. Even though the sibling relationship is sustained longer and is usually more intense, the freedom of interaction of the family style classroom compensates fairly well for this lack of siblings. Some parents wisely find other means of providing an only child with an adequate equivalence of a sibling relationship.

Once in a while a special set of circumstances in a family creates a unique piece of learning. Sara's situation is a precious example. Mrs. Crandall described Sara to me, "You know, Arthur, she behaves as though she has ten brothers and sisters. I've never seen an only child relate so well and do so well in the rough and tumble." Sara had some tomboy qualities and yet she was always gentle with others. Seldom have I seen a child who had a better disposition. How she acquired this disposition I cannot say, but no understanding of

Sara could be nearly complete unless you knew that each day she went home from nursery school to her elderly grandmother and her grandfather, who was in the terminal phase of his life. Her presence was necessary to add interest and responsibilities to their lives.

chapter 7ooooooooooooooooooooooooooo

Physical
ooooooooooooooooooooooooDifficulties

We often discover that in some children one need takes priority over others if this child is to function effectively. Perceptual difficulties are a case in point. If we expect a child to learn effectively, we should try to see that he comes to the teaching–learning situation with optimum use of his faculties. This is too often not so.

○ ADAM, *The Poker Face*
Adam was a small, thin, intense three-year-old. His relationship with his classmates was based on activity interests rather than on any bond of friendly attachment. His face showed little animation; he responded slightly, if at all, to the humor that inevitably accompanies imaginative play. Sometimes he did not follow directions. His actions were occasionally asocial. When

he decided he wanted to paint at the easel, he walked right up to it, shouldered aside the child who was there, and started painting.

When we spoke to his mother, she agreed that she had made some of these same observations. She added that he seemed to have a constant series of sore throats and colds. I suggested she take Adam for a pediatric examination, give the doctor a complete summary of our conversation, and ask whether Adam might be experiencing some impairment of hearing or other perceptual defect. The appointment was made. The examination resulted in a referral to an ear, nose and throat specialist who recommended an adenoidectomy as soon as arrangements could be made. The adenoids were severely inflamed and provision for post-operative middle ear drainage had to be made.

After the operation, Adam's hearing improved. The improvement was partial, some loss remained, but it was possible that in time there would be a total recovery. The improvement in his hearing, plus the awareness of both parents and teachers, made much difference for Adam. His nursery school experiences improved rapidly. His relationships with his classmates became friendships. The play situations, which had focused on the play objects such as blocks or painting, now included warm interactions between him, his classmates, and his teachers. Antisocial acts stopped. His reactions—especially his facial reactions—clearly showed that he fully knew what was happening or what was being said. The animation of his face was a marked contrast to the poker face, and it was a delight to see the change.

○ ARLENE, *The Shrill*

Each year we either help discover a number of hearing losses or are informed of others we did not notice. We are keenly aware that many young children have hearing difficulty, but we are still unable to catch more than a portion of those, despite our careful observation and despite our concern and awareness of the frequency of hearing loss. Parents also have difficulty and so do pediatricians. Arlene Boyd, gentle, friendly, happy, and bright, had difficulty throughout her nursery school years. Our clues to her hearing problem were the loudness and shrillness of her voice and their contrast to all other facets of her personality.

Mrs. Boyd seemed to expect our descriptions of these clues—she added that her family had a history of ear and hearing problems. When she took Arlene to the pediatrician, no loss or sign of a loss was found. Not until a year after Arlene completed nursery school was the hearing loss confirmed. As in Adam's instance, it was enlarged adenoids and an intermittent fluid retention within the ear. The hearing loss went undiagnosed because each time Arlene's hearing was tested she was well and the adenoids were treated as an entity without allowing for this side effect.

Most of the hearing losses we encounter are temporary and usually the result of adenoidal disease, impacted ear cerumen (wax), acute otitis media (ear infection), allergies, or frequent colds. One day a child hears well; on other days his hearing is impaired.

Spoken language is a key factor in early learning. Hearing impairment can make learning difficult. If parents and teachers are aware, they can compensate, and the child too can be taught to make his own adjustments. An undetected loss can have detrimental effects long after the impairment has ceased. With many children, the causative conditions subside, and the impairment stops within the first few years of school. During those years the undetected loss has made it necessary for the child to learn under a serious handicap. He misses much of what is said by the teacher and during discussions. If he doesn't learn well, it is not necessarily because he lacks the capacity. The capacity may indeed be there, but he misses whatever he does not hear. If he learns poorly, he may be judged to be a mediocre or slow student. He may accept this judgement and let it become part of his self-image. If this happens, the damage lasts long after hearing is regained.

○ BEATRICE, *The Bashful*

Beatrice was bashful. She was comfortable with other children, but when she noticed an adult observing her, she would visibly retreat from an activity. She was most bashful when an adult tried to relate directly to her. Although her nursery play was not outstanding, she had made an adequate adjustment and related well to other children. Her activity interest was also adequate. She willingly tried her hand at an ample variety of activities. When Mrs. Dean, Mrs. Crandall, and I talked about her in conference, each of us observed that we had never seen her close to any one of us when her head was not held bashfully down and her eyes averted so that she could see out through them but you could not look into them.

We agreed that we would each watch carefully to

see if we could catch her with head up and eyes open. Mrs. Dean finally did, but it took almost two weeks. "You'll never guess what I saw," she said as she came into the office. "Beatrice lifted her head and opened her eyes and, lo and behold, her eyes were way out of line." This was unexpected. A second, third, and fourth look confirmed this observation. The parents were told, and within the month Beatrice was wearing corrective glasses. Why she held her head down we will never know. Perhaps the strabismus caused double vision and she squinted to avoid the discomfort this caused. Perhaps she was keenly aware of the cosmetic appearance of crossed eyes.

Soon after she began wearing the glasses, her head came up and her eyes opened. Her school experience progressed well. She moved off her plateau and began to learn and achieve, and her relationship with adults became comfortable. She did not suddenly become a different being. She remained a pleasant, quiet child, but the bashfulness left her. She related well, was easily reached by children and adults, and readily reached out to them. Her skills, some of which could be gauged by her arts and crafts works, moved from scribbles to symbols to representational pictures, from clumsy, crude use of collage materials to skillful, imaginative works. Her ability to speak before her class changed from almost none to fully adequate.

If any single point stands out in the case of Beatrice, it is the probability that her crossed eyes were giving her a poor image of herself. I think that is the most logical explanation for her holding her head down.

I recently visited a dear friend, who in her middle years has found it necessary to have a corrective operation on malformed toes. I immediately thought of Beatrice when my friend explained that only within a month before the operation did her husband know about the malformation of the toes. She had always made a practice of covering them so that no one but she knew they were not properly formed. In her instance the malformation would have made it impossible for her to walk within a few years. In Beatrice's instance we can guess that her eye defect would have made learning increasingly difficult and have been a barrier in her relationships with others.

○ RUBY, *The Multiply Handicapped*
My most difficult parent-child separation involved a blind child who suffered from the rubella syndrome. Her name was Ruby Goode. She was referred to us by a BOCES visiting teacher who worked with multiply handicapped children. The referral was made in November. I made an appointment to speak with Mrs. Goode, Ruby, and Mrs. Marion Leavitt, the teacher.

I had no previous experience working with blind children, and at the time of the interview, Ruby was not yet able to speak. I was not sure we could work with her effectively, so at the end of our interview I asked for time to think about it.

My first step was a talk with Miss Mertis Meacham, consultant from the New York State Department of Social Welfare Commission for the Blind. She encouraged me to accept Ruby into school. She gave me books to read and agreed to work with us. I read the books and also did some serious soul searching. A pamphlet entitled *A Blind Child, Too, Can Go To Nursery School* convinced me to try. One passage, more than any other, made a particularly strong impression:

> In interpreting the child's handicap, emphasis was placed upon the fact that he is first of all a child despite his severe visual loss. His physical and emotional needs are those of any growing child, even though he may not always express them in the same way as the child with vision. He wants to be active, to have the fun of doing things, and be with people. He wants to know the feeling of a sense of power and satisfaction that comes from achievement. Because his general needs are not unlike those of other preschool children, he should not necessarily make more personal demands upon a teacher and her staff than does the aggressive, shy, or sensitive child in the group, each of whom also has specific needs.[1]

We agreed to have Ruby begin in January. In the intervening time Mrs. Leavitt and Miss Meacham began working with her at home.

When Ruby began, my uncertainty caused me to regress to the old pattern of having her mother stay in school. Mrs. Goode, who at all times did her best to help, stayed as requested but was ill at ease. On the third day Miss Meacham came. As she watched the class I told her of my uncertainty and explained that we usually insist the mother separate and go. "Well, why don't you do that now?" was her reply. I was much relieved. I realized that because of my ignorance of the problems of blindness, I was not using good judgment. I asked Mrs. Goode to leave. She willingly did, even though Ruby cried in protest.

Later that same day, Ruby, Miss Meacham, and I were outdoors with her class. The ground was covered with snow, and the kids were having fun with sleds and flying saucers. Again my uncertainty showed. I wondered aloud whether Ruby would like a sled ride. "Why don't you try and see?" Miss Meacham asked. So I tried. Ruby and I sledded down the hill. Her reaction was a combination of angry tears mixed with some evidence that she enjoyed it. Ruby's tears threw me more than did those of any of the other children. So again I wondered aloud whether, despite the tears, I hadn't discerned enjoyment. "Why don't you try it again?" asked Miss Meacham. Try again we did, and this time the enjoyment was unmistakable.

That was the beginning of a valuable experience. Ruby stayed the rest of the school year and came again for the next full school year. In the second year the Ramapo I Central School District sent William Lathrop, a school psychologist, to work with us, and Dr. Margaret M. Lawrence, a psychiatrist, began working with Ruby on a regular basis. All of us benefitted from the experience—including the children in Ruby's class. One result was the establishment of a BOCES class the next year for multiply handicapped children.

People who came to observe had a blind spot in seeing how Ruby helped her classmates. I made one discovery soon after she began. During Show and Tell, as a child was showing an umbrella, Ruby was off in a cloud. I shut my eyes and listened, trying to get some idea of what Ruby experienced. The descriptions were scant, relying more heavily on showing than on telling. They were what one might reasonably expect of a three- or four-year-old.

I felt something had to be done to include Ruby in these experiences. I interrupted and told the class what I was doing. In trying to explain how Ruby saw, I asked them to listen to the next Show and Tell with eyes closed.

Three-year-old Pete stood and held up an autograph puppy—a stuffed replica of a dachshund.

> *Me:* What did you bring?
> *Pete:* A dog.
> *Me:* What kind of a dog?
> *Pete:* White.
> *Me:* That's the color of its body. What color ears does it have?
> *Pete:* Black.
> *Me:* Can you tell me what the dog looks like?
> (Pete looked at me and shrugged his shoulders.)
> *Me:* If everybody has his eyes closed, how can you find out more about Pete's dog?
> *Henry:* We could feel with our hands.
> *Me:* That's a good idea. Let's try it.
> (The dog was passed around the class.)
> *Me:* Can anyone tell what the dog is made of?
> *Chorus:* Cloth. Cotton. Material.
> *Me:* Are its legs long or short?
> *Chorus:* Short.
> *Me:* Is its body long or short?
> *Chorus:* Long.
> *Me:* What kind of ears does it have?
> *Helen:* Floppy.

This experience demonstrated that descriptions, touch, and use of senses other than sight were needed to include Ruby in Show and Tell. Her presence was a constant reminder for each child to try harder.

A child named Hannah was Ruby's special friend. Hannah was exceptionally creative in her relationships with other children. We always depend upon the children to help each other. In Hannah the helping quality was close to ideal. She gave of herself generously with remarkable sensitivity to the needs and prerogatives of her playmates. She was Ruby's special friend. When Hannah sat making collages, Ruby often sat next to her handling scissors, glue, and hole punch. Ruby did some cutting with the scissors; this cutting and all other use of her hands and fingers were essential for the development of their strength and coordination. She didn't use the glue for gluing but enjoyed examining the shape and tactile qualities of the container. She liked to squeeze it together and feel it pop out again. Often she put it to her ear to listen as her squeeze forced air out the nozzle. Ruby would alternately use scissors, puncher, and glue, and Hannah would put and take them from her hands as she was doing her own work.

Once we watched as Hannah wheeled Ruby in the large Community Playthings carriage. Ruby indicated that she wanted to reverse their roles. We watched to see what Hannah would do. This was in the midst of free play. Many activities were taking place. Some children were building with blocks. A number were involved in varieties of art play. Several were working with hammer and nails. Some were involved in house play. How could Ruby possibly wheel Hannah without creating bedlam? Hannah figured it out without any consultation. She stopped wheeling Ruby—let her get out—put her hands on the handle bar—got into the carriage—and while Ruby pushed, Hannah controlled the speed and direction by manipulating the rear wheels. It was wonderful to behold. This and thousands of other incidents have helped me understand how resourceful children can be—if given the opportunity.

The common elements of play were the ingredients

of that relationship, but Hannah's molding of them was a fine form of creativity. This form of creativity is often ignored.

○ CHARLIE, *The Intrepid*
How well teachers learn to know each child—and the children learn to know the teachers—is illustrated by this incident between Mrs. Gilbert and Charlie.

Charlie, at birth, had severe distress of his vital functions with a low Apgar score.* His parents resourcefully and determinedly made hash of the grim prognosis given on his learning potential. By the time he began nursery school, he was well on his way to becoming a normal, healthy, intelligent child. Coincidental with his beginning school was the start of a corrective regimen for strabismus requiring the wearing of an eye patch. This was worn almost every day. This is not unusual; several children come with this problem every year. His adaptation to the patch was exceptionally good. He accepted it matter of factly. (Many children find it uncomfortable, and some pull it off every day.)

He was expected to be dull. We found him bright. His leg coordination and depth perception were not good. (The patch was enough to account for this.) He was clumsy on climbers, and Mrs. Gilbert stayed near him as he tried them out. Falls didn't deter him—he was the epitome of determination. But when he attempted to climb to the tree house, he got part way up the ladder and timidly backed down. Winter and

---

* A method devised by pediatrician Virginia Apgar, M.D., to evaluate the vitality of the newborn infant. Based on certain physical criteria, a perfectly healthy newborn will have a total of ten.

the snows halted his efforts. In spring he began again and finally made a humiliating half success—he reached the top, froze in fright, and refused to go down until Mrs. Gilbert climbed up and carried him in her arms. In mid-May he finally achieved the climb up and down the tree house by himself (with Mrs. Gilbert hovering by). In the days that followed, he rapidly became increasingly able and no longer required her protectiveness.

During a trip to a lumber yard, the kids were given a high ride on a fork lift. Charlie wanted on. Mrs. Gilbert agreed and started to accompany him. He wanted on without her. She insisted on going with him. He cried in temper, pushed her away, and refused to go unless she would stay off—they both stayed off.

Charlie's bus driver casually mentioned this episode to his mother, and a few days later Mrs. Gilbert received a most interesting feedback of the experience from Charlie's mother.

Charlie, on his own, had given her a complete account of the lumber yard trip, including his version of the fork lift incident: "I didn't go on the fork lift; Mrs. Gilbert doesn't trust me. She wouldn't let me go up unless she went with me. I wanted to go up by myself. She's always my partner when we go on a trip. All the other kids don't have teachers for partners." (As accurate as was most of his account, this last plaint omitted several interesting details. His friend Herbie was his partner on this trip. Herbie was afraid to try the fork lift. So was Mrs. Gilbert, but she was not willing for Charlie to try it without her.)

Mrs. Brown continued, "I explained that Mrs. Gilbert

was afraid that you might get frightened as you did the first time you climbed the tree house."

"That was when I was four," replied Charlie. "I'm five now, and a five-year-old isn't afraid of those things." He looked down thoughtfully for a moment, and then added, "Mrs. Gilbert doesn't watch me climb up and down the tree house anymore . . . and she doesn't watch when I climb on and off the tire swings."

Again Charlie was not completely accurate, but this time he described an important aspect of the teacher and her ever changing role as an enabler: Mrs. Gilbert continued to watch to the best of her ability but deliberately moved away as he gained ability and confidence. This was, in part, to reinforce his confidence and self-reliance. His playback is evidence of the efficacy of this methodology.

Just as Mrs. Gilbert had to know Charlie, so must each of our teachers know every child and then work with each one in all areas on the basis of where they are and where they ought next to go.

chapter 8∞∞∞∞∞∞∞∞∞∞∞∞∞∞∞∞∞∞∞∞∞∞∞

Classroom
∞∞∞∞∞∞∞∞∞∞∞∞∞∞∞∞∞∞∞∞∞∞∞∞∞Design

"This guy must be off his rocker," was the way the plumber's helper put it as he looked at the sinks he was installing in my classrooms. He didn't know who I was, and he directed his comment to me expecting an agreement. The arrangement was unusual—two sinks set in a formica frame twenty-five inches high atop a storage cabinet that jutted like a peninsula ten feet out from the wall. Closest to the wall was a conventional bathroom sink. At the open end of the peninsula was an elongated tub.

"I know it looks funny," I replied, "but that's exactly the way it's supposed to be."

I had discovered this layout at the Garden City Nursery School and realized its worth. It provides for water play and cleanup in a way that enables a child to initiate and carry through with little or no help. By way of comparison, many, if not most, classrooms provide for water play by using a small tub that must be filled and moved about by the teachers. In my set-up the child pushes down the stopper, turns on the water, and fills the tub. Other materials he needs are near and accessible to him. Since I am interested in his learning to do for himself, this is the kind of planning that enables him to do so.

More than a few observers have questioned the value of water play. Messiness bothers some adults. Nevertheless, "messing about" has attained a high status with educators who are concerned with young children. I have found it necessary to interpret its importance to many parents.

One such discussion was prompted by the parting instruction a mother gave her child, who had completed her first month of nursery school, "Remember, Lynn, when you come home I want to see your dress as clean as it is right now!"

I heard this instruction as Mrs. Martin put Lynn on the school bus. It helped me understand something that had been puzzling her teachers and myself. After we reached school, I phoned the mother.

"Mrs. Martin, in her first weeks at school Lynn's adjustment was slow. Her first real signs of progress showed when she started using art materials. She seemed delighted when she claimed her paintings and crayon drawings at the end of class. Recently she balked when given the opportunity to paint. When I heard your instructions, I realized what was on her mind."

Mrs. Martin replied "I think it is time for Lynn to learn to keep herself clean. Don't you agree?"

As gently as I could I answered, "No I don't." Then

I extolled the virtues of messing about and the glories of dirt:

"Wet art materials inevitably cause spots and stains. These are amongst the most precious kinds of messiness. To learn to create, a child needs to be comfortable with these materials. One of the most telling experiences is watching children play with fingerpaints. We use them right on the table, and they make all sorts of designs, getting into them with fingers, fingernails, flat hand, fist, up to their elbows and often beyond. We interrupt to take prints and they continue on . . .

"Sand play and water play are basic to most good nursery schools. These materials, and mud, and other forms of earth, and snow, and glorious puddles found after rain storms are natural exploration grounds for the young child. In handling these materials he is getting to know about, and getting used to, some of the most common substances that will be in his environment all his life. To understand what is happening when a child uses these materials, consider sand play and think of some of the possible learning opportunities that can come from messing around in it.

"Lynn sits and plays in the sand box. She scoops up handfuls and watches how it sifts through her fingers. She shapes it into a mountain and then pushes it down. She watches an ant crawl over it and then disappear into it. This becomes a game. She ferrets out the ant and covers him with sand and waits and watches as he extricates himself. She tries it again and again. Tired of this, she walks away and returns with a pail of water. Now she mixes sand and water and discovers that the combination makes a new kind of substance. Wet sand looks, feels, and works differently. It retains shape better. As we watch children doing this, we see them create tunnels and rivers and mountains and castles and glorious mud pies. Often they offer their pies to a teacher, and she seriously plays the game with them, remarking how good they taste. This imaginary act is typical of children's play. It could be described as a bridge Lynn crosses as she moves gracefully through the magical world of childhood in the process of growing up.

"To inhibit this form of play is to deny a child a source of learning. If he is cut off from this and other equally rich sources of learning experiences, he will lack significantly in opportunities to understand important basic information about the common elements found in his environment."

As our discussion continued, Mrs. Martin showed some acceptance of Lynn's need to use messy materials, to explore, and to get dirty. More casual dress, she decided, would be appropriate.

We are all concerned with knowing as much as possible about our environment and how to cope with it. This is as true for a child as it is for an adult. To teach him effectively, we should have a reasonably clear picture of where he is and where he seeks to go. *Explore their world—grow in curiosity and develop their individual capacities* aptly states where they are at and where they seek to go.

The young child is an explorer. The world around him, as seen through his eyes, is filled with new discoveries every day. This is a truism; it should not need explanation—but I find that it does. All too many parents and pedagogues see the child and his world through their thirty-, forty-, or fifty-year-old-eyes and judge them by inappropriate standards. A story told by the chairman of the board of a well known educational publishing house illustrates this point of view. Here is a short version:

> Some kindergartners were standing outside school during recess when they spotted an airplane. They noted the plane and began to discuss it, describing its components in technical terminology with apparent understanding. Then the bell rang, and one of them turned and said, "Come on, let's go in and string those silly beads."

The chairman's story contained far more humor than truth. It was part of a keynote address delivered at an educators' conference. He was, in effect, chiding teachers to get with it—to buy his computers and packages of programmed materials and throw away those silly beads.

A penetrating response to his gibes appears in Joseph Featherstone's *Schools Where Children Learn:*

> The extent to which existing computer-assisted instruction responds to individuals is minimal: most of the programs in use are just expensive page turners, mechanized versions of materials that could easily be put into a cheap programmed workbook. Theoretically, it's possible to create all sorts of complex, branching computer programs that can adapt to any number of responses from the student. In our present state of profound ignorance, however, it is hard for any programmer to anticipate more than a few simple alternatives. So the learner has to fit himself to the program, which is where we came in . . .
>
> Like programmed materials, a few computer methods are beginning to look promising; many

others don't. No great revolution has occurred. None seems likely. The computer technician's rule of thumb still holds good: GIGO. If you put garbage in, you get garbage out.[1]

To set up an early childhood classroom with computerized materials or programmed workbooks may be far worse than ineffective. If it is symptomatic of a total effort to teach traditional reading, writing, and arithmetic in nursery school, the child is being programmed rather than educated. He is being treated like an animal—to perform tricks that have no meaning for himself. What may result is described in a curriculum guide published by the New York State Education Department. Although this guide concerns itself with *Developing Mathematical Awareness in Prekindergarten Children,* its comments are applicable to the total conceptual abiilties of the child:

As the teacher organizes plans for an environment to foster children's mathematical activities, several threats to the plans may be encountered. Foremost among them is an anxiety to have children learn as quickly as possible. Children are sometimes rushed on to a new idea before they have grasped the old. This pressure is often caused by adults who want to show progress, and the results may be called "blurring." The child blurs the old and new into a nebulous idea, and the resulting uneasiness hinders further exploration. Gradually, he may remove himself to a safer region where his self-confidence won't be threatened. In fact, if he accumulates a goodly number of blurred ideas, he may be a candidate for remedial work in the near future.

Hundreds of children yearly have to have their faulty reading and mathematic concepts "peeled" layer by layer in a slow painstaking process until the specialist comes to the initial cause of failure.

This failure might have been prevented if the children had had time to learn, and even to over learn, simple, but important, mathematical ideas.

Closely related to "blurring" is the concept of readiness. There is fear that mathematics will be forced on children in the high chair. But readiness does not set in like a season or a day on the calendar. It is the combined result of constant daily experience and the child's maturation level. Children mentally ready will learn according to their environment and according to the guidance given them. If the teacher or parent places emphasis on the subject instead of the children, then the chances are that the child will be forced to learn before he is *ready*. If the emphasis is on the individual needs of the children, the learning can take place at appropriate moments.

Another threat to the child's learning process is a lack of manipulative materials. Children seldom differentiate between work and play. They work hard at play and play hard at work. As they pit themselves against everything in their environment, there should be an abundance of material. Each learning activity whether planned, spontaneous, formal, or informal should be saturated with materials, aids, or devices. In this phase of involvement, the task of supplying the proper materials at the proper time is crucial.[2]

The classroom designed as an effective tool allows a child his own play choices from a variety of manipulative materials. To start where he is at, the materials should represent familiar aspects of his daily environment including home, family, community, outdoors, vehicles, and animals.

The materials are placed to allow him complete opportunity to organize and develop his own play. Watching a child paint at an easel illustrates how this principle is carried out. He begins by taking a smock from a hook near the drying rack. The smocks' styles are varied, but he can manipulate any of them. Newsprint is draped over the drying rack. He peels off a sheet and secures it to the easel. A crayon conveniently dangles from the easel so that he may use it to print his name. If he can't print, a teacher does this for him. Brushes sit in the paint cups—one for each color. If he mixes colors or brushes either by intent or accident, this is expected and desired. He removes the

finished painting and hangs it on the drying rack. If paint has dripped on the floor, he wipes it up with a small hand mop. Then he takes off and hangs up the smock. Not every child can do all this. A teacher helps occasionally but tries to do *for* him no more than is necessary.

The way children use the materials demonstrates their need to repeat experiences over and over again. Recently I joined Amy, Beth, and Carl as they sat at a table doing a See-Into Puzzle about a kitchen. Under each puzzle piece is an illustration of what might usually be found inside. Behind a kitchen cabinet door, for example, are plates, mugs, a pitcher, and bowls. I asked, "Who can guess what's behind this door?" Their faces lit up and the guessing began. I meant only to show them a new way to use the puzzle, but they made me play the game three times before I was allowed to relinquish my role to Amy. Even then their play continued, and each took a turn as questioner as the others guessed again.

chapter 9 ∞∞∞∞∞∞∞∞∞∞∞∞∞∞∞∞∞∞∞∞∞

Language
∞∞∞∞∞∞∞∞∞∞∞∞∞∞∞∞∞∞∞∞∞∞∞∞∞∞∞∞∞ Skills

Our placement of books in the classroom is analogous to an artist's use of highlights. Just as his highlights accentuate and give dimension to his painting, so do the books accentuate and give dimension to our classroom experiences. When it is winter, books and pictures about winter are prominently displayed. This is done for all seasons and for the trips we take and for holidays and other topics we seek to highlight. As we read the books that relate to current experiences, they add depth and dimension. What is seen or experienced becomes better understood, and interest in the books grows because they are relevant and extend experiences still further.

Placing books all around the room makes them easily accessible and encourages the children to take and "read" them whenever they please. They do this frequently. There is also a book rack and a phonograph placed near a rug to form a reading area. The rack contains book and record sets. The children can operate the phonograph themselves and follow the text or the pictures as the record plays.

Several years ago I used the term "readiness" when describing what we were doing with the children in reading, math, and the sciences. Now I say we are teaching reading, math, and the sciences, because I think this is exactly what we are doing. I hastily add that, "We must remember that we are teaching three-, four- and five-year-olds, in terms of where they are at and where they ought to be able to go." This approach makes us more effective because the reading experience is part of language development—and so are math and science. By recognizing that we are involved with reading right here and now, we can identify and develop appropriate developmental skills. Motivation and language development are our first concerns. We try to help children become motivated to use speech in a variety of situations and to love books. The most important motivation should come from the child himself.

Need and desire are two factors teachers should understand and use. Need comes in many forms: a child's need to have his hunger satisfied, his need to eliminate body.wastes, his need to be reassured when he fears, to receive attention and affection, to express wants, ideas, or feeling, to relate to other human beings, to learn, to inquire. This list could go on and on in terms of basic common human needs. Needs should be realized and utilized in the teaching–learning process.

A child measures himself by comparison with his peers. Allowing for a range of aptitudes, he feels that what they can do, he should be able to do. If his peers can speak, then he should be able to speak. They will require him to do so, unless they are given to understand that he lacks this capacity. His desires to relate, to play, and to express himself are constantly required in the learning experience. As teachers, we evaluate his needs and adjust our roles to facilitate their fulfillment. This is what Mrs. Rosenthal and Mrs. Lawrence did when they worked with Lionel, the boy who could speak but wouldn't. We try to do it with every child. This means that our role in helping them in their language development requires us to evaluate where they are and then, in our interactions and conversations with them, to try to help them consolidate important factors such as vocabulary, concepts, or awareness of sounds and to challenge them to move on.

To teach children to love books may sound specious —but we really do try. We have assembled a large selection of good books. We use them effectively to help children learn more about what they are seeing and doing—to increase their awareness of people, places, and things they have not seen before—to enjoy—the more belly laughs we have reading books together, the more likely children are to be motivated to look to books for more enjoyment.

Several years ago during one of our parents' meetings, a mother suggested that a trip to a library might add to this effort of fostering love of books. It seemed like a good idea, and I promised to give it further thought. Since the mother who made the suggestion was a former children's librarian, I phoned her several days later and asked whether she could make some inquiries at local libraries to see if they would be willing to host eight classes of nursery school children. She not only began the arrangements for the visits but also made a list of suggestions of things the children might learn that would give them a good first impression of a library.

In briefing me about our prospective visit, the mother suggested I especially try to arrange one at the Pearl River Public Library because its children's librarian, Miss Carolyn E. Johnson, was particularly good. Since our school is located in Suffern, I anticipated that our choices of trip sites would be libraries that were closer to us. The Suffern Free library readily scheduled several visits but suggested we try arranging others elsewhere because it could not comfortably schedule eight. The next closest library reluctantly agreed to schedule one. Thus necessity prodded me into calling Pearl River:

"Miss Johnson," I began, "this is Arthur Gilbert calling. I am the director of a nursery school in Suffern. I am calling to see if we can arrange to have several of our classes visit your library so that they may learn what a library is like."

"What a wonderful idea!" responded Miss Johnson.

The rest of our conversation was devoted to arranging the dates and my expressing some ideas on what we hoped to accomplish.

Miss Johnson proved to be as good as her word. The visits with her were indeed "a wonderful idea."

When the children arrived at the library, she greeted them and suggested they take off their jackets, put them on a table, and then sit on the floor in the corner of the children's library. When they were seated, she began, "I think we are going to have some fun."

Then she stopped and looked around absentmindedly. "You know, I thought I had brought some friends with me."

She continued to look about, and their heads turned to join her in the search. "Oh here they are," her voice showed her relief at having found them. "Here are my friends!" she said as she picked up three books, and the children burst into laughter.

"But they are my friends!" she protested, as if hurt by their laughter. Then in a calmer tone that seemed to gather them into her confidence, she revealed a special secret, "Look at the shelves all around this room."

As their heads turned she asked, "Did you ever see so many books? All the other rooms of this library are also filled with books. Every day hundreds of people come to read these books. Some they read here. Some they take home and read."

Then she walked to the shelf where the unabridged edition of the *Random House Dictionary of the English Langauge* lay open ready for use. She lifted it holding it open. They were impressed by its size. "This is one of the biggest books. It has in it all of the words we speak from little ones like a−an−it−the−boy−girl−to such big ones as pneumonoultramicroscopicsilicovolcanoconiosis."

With that she put the dictionary down and put her hand to her chest as if to catch her breath and then added, "How about that?"

This they found very funny. Then she added, "You know when I go home after I've worked all day, I like to sit in a big comfortable chair after supper and read a book. In the books I read, I meet interesting people, or I do things I've never done before, or sometimes I go to far away places I've never seen before. And just think—as I read a book, I can climb to the top of the highest mountain—and not break my leg—or I can go all around the world and not even have to pay airplane fare."

Then she offered to read to them, and they readily assented. She read *It Looked Like Spilt Milk* [1] by Charles Shaw. They enjoyed its whimsy and humor.

Her timing was beautiful. Before they knew what was happening, she was showing them "a machine that eats paper." This was the Gaylord Charger, which nibbles the edges of the due date cards. "This drawer is the stomach of the machine," she explained as she pulled out the catch bucket filled with clippings and emptied them into an envelope saying, "You can have these to take back to school. Maybe you can use them on collages."

Pointing to an oil painting that hung on the wall, she asked, "How would you like to give that to your grandmother for a present?" They thought this a great idea. "Well, you can," she continued. "If you come here with mother or daddy, we'll let you take this picture to hang in your grandmother's home for a whole month. Or if you like, one of these." She pointed to others on the wall. "You can take any of these to grandmother."

"Did you know we have a detective in this room?" They were perplexed. They looked all around the room and saw nobody who could possibly be a detective. "Here is our detective," she said tapping her index finger on the card catalog. "When I want to find a book, I look in here, and this detective tells me where it is. Want to see how it works? Give me the name of a book, and this detective will tell me where to find it."

Magically she produced several books requested by first looking in the card catalog and then walking directly to the location of the book. They were duly impressed. She then read another story, *Who's There, Open the Door*[2] by Bruno Munari. As she read, she piqued their curiosity by peeking ahead to see the pictures of the characters they sought to identify.

Several days after the trip the children were busy collaborating on a book of their art works to send to Miss Johnson as a thank-you. One child insisted that he decorate his collage with some of the clippings from "the machine that eats paper."

In my personal thank you to Miss Johnson I wrote, "I'm sure they didn't learn the Dewey Decimal System, but after that trip they are almost certain to remember that a library is a wonderful place."

In one of his earliest works, *The Child and the Curriculum*, Dewey stated a key point that is basic to his philosophy of education:

. . . the lack of any organic connection with what the child has already seen and felt and loved makes the material purely formal and symbolic. . . . A symbol which is induced from without, which has not been led up to in preliminary activities, is, as we say, a *bare* or *mere* symbol; it is dead and barren. Now, any fact, whether of arithmetic, or geography, or grammar, which is not led up to and into out of something which has previously occupied a significant position in the child's life for its own sake, is forced into this position. . . . The clue being lacking, it remains an idle curiosity, to fret and obstruct the mind, a dead weight to burden it.

The second evil in this external presentation is lack of motivation. There are not only no facts or truths which have been previously felt as such with which to appropriate and assimilate the new, but there is no craving, no need, no demand. . . .[3]

Effective early childhood teachers work from this base of understanding. This is one reason I find it essential to have an extensive variety of good books readily available *in* the classroom. Books allow us to relate our reading to current concerns or immediate or impending experiences. They enable us to bind symbol together with the reality of the child's experiences.

A particularly effective reading experience occurred when I took two glowering antagonists, who had previously been steadfast friends, and read to them *Let's be Enemies.*[4] The relevance could not possibly be missed. By the time the characters in the story were ready to relent and share a pretzel, the real life antagonists, each of whom was perched on one of my knees, were sheepishly smiling at each other, and so were the others in their class. When we discusssed the story after the reading, we all agreed that we each had differences and disagreements but enjoyed making up.

It is interesting to note that I usually begin this book by asking whether anyone knows what an enemy is. After I get a satisfactory definition, I then ask, "Does anyone here have an enemy?" The room immediately grows brighter from the glow of their halos. Not a one admits to having an enemy. After some discussion, one brave one remembers, "I don't like Freddy. He always wants to fight." That opens a flood of confessions. Their memories soon allow them each to recall *bona fide* enemies. Those who can't readily recall one can usually be expected to produce an imaginary one for this occasion.

This is a good illustration of their developing sense of propriety. With the clearest of consciences I reassure them that it is perfectly all right to disagree. This is the least I can do to undo some of the damage done by elders who preach to them the gospel of the three monkeys—*hear no evil, see no evil, speak no evil.*

Sometimes I suspect that *taste no evil* is also included. This happens when I read them *Green Eggs and Ham*.[5] I like to stop at the page that shows the face of the much besieged character as he finally begins to taste the often offered green eggs and ham. "Do any of you make a face like that when your mommy asks you to taste something?"

As if they were a Greek chorus, they say in unison, with a tone of solemn and earnest conviction, "Oh no!" But again, with a little coaxing someone breaks down and confesses, "I don't like plain milk—but I drink chocolate milk." Even a little crack like that is apt to break the dam and release another flood of confessions.

We long ago proved children's reluctance to taste something new. Several years ago in the middle of winter doldrums, we read this story and at its finish paraded a platter of green eggs into the classroom and offered everyone a taste. This was high comedy. There were all sorts of reactions. Its prime purpose was to provide one of several bright spots in the middle of the grey confinement of winter. It also happens to be good pedagogy, effectively relating symbol to experience.

Discussions that stem from stories are one of several ways we encourage conversation. The importance of language necessitates that we consciously provide several ways of encouraging speech and then use each of these ways as effectively as we can. Show and Tell is another way. In some instances a child who is not yet able to Tell is willing to Show. We encourage his inclinations. The teachers have become adept at evoking conversations from children who need much help and challenging each child appropriately. Here are some sequences illustrating some of the variety in Show and Tell:

Teacher: Albie, tell me something about your yellow tractor. Incidentally, how did I know this belongs to Albie?
Benny: 'Cause Albie always brings in tractors and trucks.
Suzy: And cars.
Teacher: Yes, Albie always brings in cars, trucks, or anything with wheels. Albie, tell me something about your tractor.
Albie: It's a car.
Teacher: How many wheels does it have? Let's count them.
Albie: (Counting as the teacher touches each wheel) One – two – three – four – five – six.
Teacher: That was very good.
Albie. Seven – in the middle.
Teacher: What do you call that wheel?
Albie: The steering wheel.
Fran: My brother has that tractor too.
Teacher: What does this tractor do?
Albie: Build a road.
Teacher: What is this made of? (Albie is perplexed.)
Teacher: (Tapping it with her fingernail) What does this sound like?
Albie: Metal.
Teacher: Let's find out whether it has any iron or steel on it. Albie, you take the magnet and test it to see if it has any iron or steel.

Albie: (Guessing) On the wheel.
Teacher: Try it. Put the magnet on the wheel. Does it stick?
Albie: No. (Pointing) I think that thing there.
Teacher: That's called the axle. Does it stick?
Albie: It sticks!
Teacher: What does that mean.
Albie: It has iron.

Because Albie is not overly verbal, the teacher carefully listens to him and uses her questions to draw him out. When he is encouraged, he proves that he knows quite a bit about his tractor. Another more talkative child then raises his hand:

Teacher: Our friend Buddy has a Tell.
Buddy: One of my cars has iron but not all of it.
Teacher: Not the whole car?
Buddy: About half of it.
Teacher: What part has iron?
Buddy: The little things on the wheels. The caps on the wheels has iron.
Teacher: The hubcaps?
Buddy: Yes.

Visits with cousins are a frequent topic, including some that are in only the wishing stage:

Cheryl: Some day I'm going to visit my cousin Nancy.
Teacher: Are you?
Cheryl: She gots two Sesame books.
Teacher: What are they about?
Cheryl: One has letters and one has pictures.
Teacher: Do you remember the letters?
Cheryl: I don't remember all of them, but I'll tell you ones I remember.
Teacher: All right. Which do you remember?

Cheryl: G, N, I, E, J.
Teacher: G, N, I, E, J?
Cheryl: and B.
Teacher: Can you think of a word that begins with B?
Cheryl: Well I remember S. That has a lot of words.
Teacher: All right, tell me some that begin with S.
Cheryl: I know a lot of them.
Teacher: Let's think of names.
Jake: Susie.
Teacher: Susie, Yes.
Cheryl: I'm not going to tell names, I'm going to tell different words.
Teacher: All right Cheryl.
Cheryl: Snow.
Teacher: Snow is a great word. I'm thinking of something you put on your feet. What do you put on your feet that begins with S.
Cheryl: Socks.
Teacher: Very good.
Kathy: Santa Claus.
Hope: Sleigh.
Teacher: I'm thinking of another word that is like a sleigh and rhymes with bed.
Freddie: Sled.

Cheryl's imaginary visit with her cousin led to a discussion of letters and thence to a game about initial sounds. The children's enjoyment of word play is obvious. We recently acquired *Tikki Tikki Tembo*,[6] a folktale about why Chinese give their children short names. The denouement results from the necessity of pronouncing the name of a child who has fallen into a well. To summon the rescuers they must be informed that, "Tikki tikki tembo—no sa rembo-chari bari ruchi—pip peri pembo has fallen into the well."

To shorten or leave out the name would be irreverent. Needless to say, Tikki tikki tembo—no sa rembo —chari bari ruchi—pip peri pembo almost drowns.

Curiosity led me to ask the teachers of the eight classes what happened when they read this story. Each replied that the children had, without prompting, automatically joined in whenever she read *Tikki—tikki tembo—no sa rembo—chari bari ruchi—pip peri pembo*.

This is not an isolated experience. It happens whenever there is a repetitive tongue or titillating phrase. Some who are most eager to sing songs with catchy phrases or imitative sounds are children who have difficulty with sounds.

The enjoyment children show might well indicate how much they need these opportunities to play with word sounds. Here is another instance where an adult, having long ago acquired his skill, is not aware of how complicated it is for the beginner. The frequency of speech defects in young children should suffice to make teachers aware and prompt them to find ways of helping. Fascination with word sounds, I feel, accounts for the popularity of children's stories and songs that have elements of rhyme and alliteration.

Whenever a teacher reads *Millions of Cats*,[7] inevitably a spontaneous chorus chants:

"Hundreds of cats,
  Thousands of cats,
  Millions and billions and trillions of cats."

We are also greatly concerned about comprehension. Show and Tell also provides word play opportunities that build this skill. We can usually anticipate such a game when a child begins his turn by walking up to the teacher clutching a paper bag:

Teacher: Let's see if we can guess what Elliot has in his bag. Give us some clues Elliot.

Elliot: It has a head. It has eyes. A tail. A mouth—and a wheel.

Teacher: One wheel?

Elliot: Four! (He is quite pleased with himself.)

Teacher: Does it have anything special like the trunk of the elephant?

Elliot: A mouth.

Teacher: You already told us it had a mouth. (They look into the bag together.)

Teacher: (Pointing) What about these?

Elliot: Stripes!

Different children: A zebra!
                      A tiger!
                      A cat!

Elliot: It's a cat.

Teacher: Well, it is in the cat family, but it is a tiger. (At this point Elliot opened his bag and pulled out a toy tiger on wheels.)

Comprehension is helped by both the act of describing and the act of deducing. The preceding description was based on physical characteristics. Here's one based on function:

Fern: (Holding up a small bag) Guess!

Teacher: Is it more than one thing?

Fern: Yes. You can make anything you want—faces, bodies—like blocks but not . . .

Teacher: What shape is it?

Fern: Round faces like fat head, skinny head. . . . .

Teacher: Is it hard or soft?

Fern: Hard and soft.

Adam: People?

Fern: You can make people.

Staci: Shapies?

Fern: No. (At this point the children gave up, and

Fern identified the hidden object as a Snap-on Game, a toy that allows one to combine different features of people or animals and snap them together).

The teacher followed this exchange by helping the children through some evaluation of the Snap-On game. Some time was spent identifying colors, some in identifying which features belonged to which animals. The confusing answer "hard and soft" was clarified. The teacher pointed out that it could be called either because the surfaces of the objects were hard, but since some of them were hollow they could be squeezed and thus considered soft.

Poetry adds something very special to our introductory reading course. Well-selected poems tell about all sorts of things in ways that show how well words can paint pictures, describe feelings or awaken children's minds to the magical qualities in things that they had not seen as well before.

This poem by Langston Hughes [8] makes a wonderful springboard to a discussion:

> I loved my friend.
> He went away from me.
> There's nothing more to say.
> The poem ends,
> Soft as it began—
> I loved my friend.

To help children learn how to handle their feelings, one must begin with some expression of emotions. It is not always necessary to wait for an incident. The teacher can use a poem like this to open up talk about a feeling that everyone experiences—the loss of the companionship of someone we love. It takes much time, experience, and many lessons to learn how to handle separations. Through this kind of discussion a child can learn that others experience this same kind of sadness. He may learn of some ways to compensate —perhaps the fun of reunions, perhaps phone conversations, maybe correspondence through his parents. Maybe he can do some form of correspondence himself. He can at least discover that there is still a measure of happiness to be found in recollections of fun that he and his friend had together.

The descriptive quality of poetry can help a child learn how well words paint pictures. On a rainy day, try this one by Lillian Moore: [9]

> *OUTSIDE*
> I
> am inside
> looking outside
> at the pelting
> rain—
> where
> the outside world
> is melting
> upon my
> window
> pane.

Here is one everyone should know. It helps us see better something as familiar as the air we breathe.

> *THE STAR*
> Twinkle, twinkle, little star,
> How I wonder what you are
> Up above the world so high,
> Like a diamond in the sky.

When the blazing sun is set,
And the grass with dew is wet,
Then you show your little light,
Twinkle, twinkle, all the night

Then the traveler in the dark
Thanks you for your tiny spark;
He could not see which way to go
If you did not twinkle so.

In the dark blue sky you keep
And often through my curtains peep,
For you never shut your eye
Till the sun is in the sky.

As your bright and tiny spark
Lights the traveler in the dark,
Though I know not what you are.
Twinkle, twinkle, little star.

Sometimes I ask the children to close their eyes and try to imagine what the poet is saying. If I do this when reading "The Star," I finish by showing the accompanying illustration in our copy of *First Poems of Childhood*,[10] illustrated by Tasha Tudor. The imagery of the poems and their illumination through the paintings of Miss Tudor are likely to stir imaginations within the children. This poem has been set to music, and the children enjoy learning and singing the lesser known verses.

chapter 10 ○○○○○○○○○○○○○○○○○○○○○○○○

Imparting
○○○○○○○○○○○○○○○○○○○○○○○○○○○○○○○○○ Values

When I speak of fostering love in the young child, I am aware that his ability cannot be expected to have all the qualities of mature love. This applies whether this is love of people or of things such as books. He is, nevertheless, learning love right along with all else that matters to him. How he feels about people who are different from him will be a part of that learning. The attitudes of his parents and teachers will have impact on his forming values.

Other influencing factors loom large in his everyday experiences. When we consider the possible impact of such forces as television, movies, indiscriminately selected books, random conversations that reach the child's ears, and tasteless advertising, we realize we cannot stand idly by and allow these to be his only teachers. The bias, the stereotyping, and the downright falseness they propagate and perpetuate do incalculable mischief. The National Association for Better Broadcasting, a watchdog group composed of concerned educators, makes an annual evaluation of commercial television programs for children. Here is a sampling of some popular programs, including some that reflect bad taste and lack of real concern for children: [1]

ADAM 12—Police portrayed as competent human beings. Constructive for younger viewers. A good starting point for discussions across the generation gap.

ALIAS SMITH AND JONES—A western similar to the old Maverick series. Callous, sadistic. Brutality treated in a light-hearted way. The violence and the distortion of social values represented by heroes who are outside the law make this confusing and unsuitable for children.

ARNIE—A funny show with real people who make real-life decisions. Always in good taste.

BATMAN—When this series was produced for ABC, the network claimed that it was basically satiric humor, but children do not respond to *Batman* as funny. The lure is violence and morbid suspense. The show disparages social values. Now aired daily during children's hours by some stations, it's more objectionable than ever.

THE FLINTSTONES—Wily women outwit the male characters. Ingenious animation of animals, very poor human relationships.

HOGAN'S HEROES—An irresponsible mockery of documented historical tragedy. The Nazis were not comic buffoons, nor were World War II prisoners a joke. This is an unwholesome show that illustrates war as a setting for fun and harmless adventure.

THE INVADERS—Tense melodrama. Hostile creatures from a doomed planet invade earth. Not for children.

JUVENILE JURY—An explosive show that downgrades children by encouraging them to be smart-alecky and cute. Ugly sort of adult attitude, which laughs *at* children, not with them.

CAPTAIN KANGAROO—This is still one of commercial TV's few responsible shows for preschoolers. Bob Keeshan is to be applauded for his new policy of not doing commercials. The show is resourceful in its approach to many aspects of a child's world. It includes an articulate, charming black character. Humor and warm personal relationships.

LASSIE—Over-suspensful story situations. NABB suggests that parents check the impact of *Lassie* on their children, and bear in mind that the program is designed for family viewing.

LOST IN SPACE—Poor quality science fiction. Bad family pattern for young viewers—children are disobedient, care is not taken by adults, and stories are left hanging. Nothing to recommend.

MAGILLA GORILLA CARTOONS—Noisy heavy-handed cartoons. Mediocre and insensitive. Objectionable for children.

MILTON THE MONSTER—Tasteless and grotesque animated monsters. Objectionable.

NATIONAL GEOGRAPHIC—Outstanding programs with great appeal for the whole family.

ROMPER ROOM—Show content varies from city to city. Constructive aspects are overshadowed by excessive commericalism. An investigator for Action for Children's television picked up this bit delivered by the "teacher" in Bangor, Maine: "God is great. God is good. Let us thank him for our food. And now you may drink your Tropicanna Orange Juice from the Pleasant Hill Dairy."

TOM AND JERRY CARTOONS—Much action, little plot; ridicules authority. Unsuitable.

WILD KINGDOM—Wild life photographed beautifully in its wilderness surroundings. Entertaining, with real values for all.

WILD WILD WEST—Highly objectionable. Contains some of the most sadistic and frightening sequences ever produced.

Violence is a frequent theme, and often the greatest violence is the way other ethnic groups are treated. After seeing the typical western fanfare, a child is likely to picture the Indian as a savage who lies in wait to surprise wagon trains of settlers heading West and cruelly kills helpless women and children.

Even the unexplored reaches of outer space are being exploited to prejudice young minds. Much of the TV science fiction pictures the vast unknown as filled with terrifying, surrealistic monsters. It makes me uncomfortable to realize that we are projecting mankind's fears and follies into outer space.

Early in our school year we begin to provide antidotes to counter these poisons. Our "social science" studies go on all year to help children towards more conscious awareness and understanding of others in his environment, community, and world. *Pennies for UNICEF* provides the thematic stimulus for our first foray. I time our Parents' Meeting for early October so that we may go this route together on Halloween. I tell

them that we will enable the children to participate in this project making it clear that this should not be regarded as a high powered fund-raising project. The opportunities it provides to open up their awareness of different peoples and countries and to introduce them to an experience of helping others are the real lessons.

We lead up to this experience by reading books about people in different countries and also about some of the varieties of people in America. We sing songs from all around the world. Show and Tell becomes sprinkled with memorabilia from other countries including dolls, costumes, and artifacts. We display UNICEF posters and explain that the pennies are needed to buy milk, food, medicine, vaccines, and educational services for children in more than one hundred different countries. We show them the filmstrip *Faces and Places in UNICEF's World*,[2] adapting it to their understanding.

Helping children learn to understand and accept differences is a major thrust in this sequence. By providing excellent springboards for discussions, books enable the children to discern some of the differences between peoples of different countries.

The portrayal of an Indian youth and his family in the story *Little Wolf*[3] is much fairer than the usual stereotype. Illustrations are important in this and in most other children's books. Learning to respect differences among people is this story's central point. Little Wolf sets himself apart from other youths by refusing to learn to hunt. His father and others in the tribe at first rebuff him but eventually respect him for his desire and aptitude to become a healer.

An effective storyteller can use this book in many different ways. Here are some topics that occur to me as I leaf through the pages: (1) Indian homes, (2) Indian foods and food preparation, (3) Indian artifacts, (4) Physical characteristics of the Indian, (5) Indian dress, (6) Indian family life, (7) How the Indian lives with his environment, (8) The importance of hunting in Indian life, (9) Plants and animals Little Wolf knows, and (10) Little Wolf's way—was he right in choosing to be different?

From its illustrations and our discussions of this story the children may begin to develop a more enlightened view of Indians. The conflict that arises from Little Wolf's refusal to become a hunter adds special interest.

It stresses the individual differences that are to be found in any group.

Another story that does this particularly well is *Crow Boy*.[4] It is interesting to note that it was in part dedicated to, "Takeo Isonaga who appears in this story as a teacher named Isobe." The children readily identify with the story's characters because they are in a classroom situation. Crow Boy is the different child. For five school terms he is abused and ridiculed. He is labeled stupid and slowpoke. In the sixth year Mr. Isobe arrives and takes over the instruction of the class. Through his interest and relationship, he helps the other children understand and appreciate Crow Boy's special qualities. He turns around the rebuffs that were caused by Crow Boy's strange ways. The others learn that each day this strange child travels to school from a far and lonely place where his family farms the land. His way of life gives him a store of knowledge about plants and animals and the ways of the woods, fields, and mountains. Mr. Isobe's ability to see something special in Crow Boy's difference is a quality that each of us should learn.

If the songs, stories, discussions, and participation in *Pennies for UNICEF* moves the children to a beginning awareness and appreciation of the many different people who live on this earth, then we truly have raised an enriching fund.

chapter 11 ○○○○○○○○○○○○○○○○○○○○○○○○○

Music and
○○○○○○○○○○○○○○○○○○○○○○○○○○○○○○○○○○○○○○Art

One song published in book form is *Over in the Meadow*.[1] Our copy is illustrated by Feodor Rojankovsky. It is a counting song as well as a fine lesson in animal families, animal homes, and meadow ecology. Its "pictures are filled with the wonder and beauty of meadow life from earliest morning till the end of day." We have an ecology lesson as we enjoy ourselves singing this song.

We sing for enjoyment. Learning follows naturally. Word play abounds in songs. Some of it imitates animal sounds as in "Old MacDonald" or "The Greenberry Tree." In some songs we mimic nonsense phrases such as:

> If you're happy and you know it
> Go inkus godinkus
>   or

Put your fingers on your shoe
And we'll all go boo-hoo-hoo.

For some reason the more plaintive my boo-hoo-hoo, the merrier is the childrens!

The "Bus Song," which can be learned instantly, involves hand play as well as imitative sounds. As the wheels on the bus go round, round, round, the children's arms vigorously inscribe circles in the air. Then their rrum-rrum-rrum imitates the revving of the motor. Their hands push the horn, and their voices sing beep, beep, beep. The wipers go swish, swash, swish, and hands and arms inscribe arcs on imaginary windshields. They resolutely control the steering wheel as the driver drives all around and bounce vigorously as the seats on the bus go up and down.

To pass that song by without occasionally opening a discussion about one of its descriptive passages would be a waste of good material. Sometimes after we sing "The blinkers on the bus go blink, blink, blink," I add, "The signals on the bus go wink, wink, wink." This is fun because winking is not easy for this age child, and yet they like to try. So we take time out for wink demonstrations.

The young child's interpretations of the bus' working parts reveal his qualifications as half magician, half scientist. When I asked a class to explain how the signals work, one child replied, "When you turn the switch, it makes electricity. That's how we get light." He was not completely sure of himself so he then turned to me and asked, "That's right, isn't it?" I assured him he had the right idea but asked whether he thought the switch made the electricity. He did. I explained that the switch didn't make the electricity; it just stopped or allowed the flow.

I tried to explain it further by comparing the switch to a faucet. As I turned the faucet open and closed, the water flowed and stopped. "The water," I explained, "is there all the time. When the faucet is shut, it stops the flow, When it is open, it allows the flow." I then showed them how this works by using a transparent pipette on a small reservoir—with my fingers acting as the faucet.

Their answer to the question, "Where is the motor?" demonstrated that their limited experience has produced limited insight:

> "In the trunk"
> "Nooo silly. It's in the front."
> "In my daddy's Volks it's in the back."
> "It's under the hood."

On lights one insisted, "It comes from the light bulbs." Another corrected him "Noooo, silly, it comes from electricity."

The source of music itself is more reassuring. Ruth Crawford Seeger says it well in her book *American Folk Songs for Children:*

This music has been a natural part of work, play, sleep, fun, ridicule, love, death. It has grown out of and passed through many ways of living and doing. Facts and fantasies cling to it from its wandering. It knows and tells what people have thought about the ways of living and the things that happened. Through it one can grow in intimate appreciation of the railroads it helped build, the cotton it helped pick, the ships it helped sail, the land stretches it made less lonely.[2]

There appears to be a growing trend to integrate curriculum. Music fits perfectly in this schema. In early childhood classrooms it is a practice of long standing to teach about the world around us through song. Railroad songs are an especially appropriate example.

Things that go fascinate the young child. These include many vehicles from wheel toys to rocket ships. Railroads continue to rate high in a child's interest, despite their present demise from competing forms of transportation.

"I Been Workin' on the Railroad" is probably one of the best known songs. Almost everyone seems to know it, yet its origin is unknown. It tells something about the life of the Negro railroad hand in the South. The ballad "John Henry" tells about "a six foot tall, 200 pound black man 'of pure African blood'— (who) could outsing and outdrive any other man on the job." Through these songs we learn about the men who built our railroads, and John Henry swinging his twenty-pound hammer takes his place alongside such folk heroes as Johnny Appleseed and Paul Bunyon. Ezra Jack Keats has written and illustrated a children's book entitled *John Henry: An American Legend.*[3] It enables children to learn through song, story, and pictures about the titanic labors of the workers who laid the tracks and tunnelled through mountains to build the railroads that opened up the West.

"Casey Jones" tells of the brave engineer and his exploits on the Cannonball Express. "The Wabash Cannon Ball" tells the glories of "the most wondrous railroad in the world." "The Big Rock Candy Mountain," which enjoys celebrity as a children's song, is the work and story of the hobo, another famous railroad character.

To my mind the efficacy of song in the learning experiences of children deserves recognition equal to manipulation in mathematical concept development. This is my belief, but I cannot prove it. To strengthen my contention, consider another phase of music—the activity record. One of the best known and most widely used is coincidentally "Train to the Zoo." [4] The combination of word imagery, imitative sounds, rhythm, and tonality can compare with the physical manipulation of objects. The chorus of the title song enables a child to identify himself with the sounds of the train whistle and locomotion, and acting out allows him to physically imitate the train leaving the station:

> Choo - choo
> Choo - choo
> Chug - chug, chug - chug
> Chug - chug, chug - chug
> Chugga - chugga, - chugga - chugga
> Chugga - chugga - chugga - chugga
> Train to the zoo.

In the last line he identifies with the conductor calling out the station.

It is easy to understand how well this record enhances an actual trip to the zoo. In addition to the train song, it contains wonderfully descriptive songs about the monkey, the bear, the seal and the elephant. In slow rhythm and dolorous tonality they sing.

Swaying, swaying
Elephant's trunk is swaying;
Elephant's eating his hay.
Clomping, clomping—
Elephant's feet are clomping;
Elephant's going away.

As I assess the impact of this kind of experience, I am reminded of Erik Erikson's sequence in which he recounts how Tom Sawyer, laboring at whitewashing a fence, observed the coming of his friend Ben Rogers:

He took up his brush and went tranquilly to work. Ben Rogers hove in sight presently—the very boy, of all boys, whose ridicule he had been dreading. Ben's gait was the hop-skip-and jump—proof enough that his heart was light and his anticipations high. He was eating an apple, and giving a long, melodious whoop, at intervals, followed by a deep-toned ding-dong-dong, ding-dong-dong, for he was personating a steamboat. As he drew near, he slackened speed, took the middle of the street, leaned far over to starboard and rounded to ponderously and with laborious pomp and circumstance—for he was personating the Big Missouri, and considered himself to be drawing nine feet of water. He was boat and captain and engine-bells combined, so he had to imagine himself standing on his own hurricane-deck giving the orders and executing them:
. . . 'Stop the stabboard! Ting-a-ling-ling! Stop the labboard! Come ahead on the stabboard! Stop her! Let your outside turn over slow! Ting-a-ling-ling! Chow-ow-ow! Get out that head-line! *Lively* now! Come—out with your spring-line—what're you about there! Take a turn round that stump with the bight of it! Stand by that stage, now—let her go! Done with the engines, sir! Ting-a-ling! Sh't! sh't! sh't!' (trying the guage cocks).

Tom went on whitewashing—paid no attention to the steamboat. Ben stared a moment, and then said:

"Hi-*yi! You're* up a stump, ain't you! . . . You got to work, hey?"

My clinical impression of Ben Rogers is a most favorable one, and this on all three counts: organism, ego, and society. For he takes care of the body by munching an apple; he simultaneously enjoys imaginary control over a number of highly conflicting items (being a steamboat and parts thereof, as well as being the captain of said steamboat, and the crew obeying said captain); while he loses not a moment in sizing up social reality when, on navigating a corner, he sees Tom at work. By no means reacting as a steamboat would, he knows immediately how to pretend sympathy though he undoubtedly finds his own freedom enhanced by Tom's predicament.[5]

Erikson then theorizes, "that the child's play is the infantile form of the human ability to deal with experience by creating model situations and to master reality by experiment and planning."

To tie my postulation to Erikson's theory, one need merely accept musical activities as one form of "model situations."

When I sing with the children, our interaction has a quality that one can almost taste. Gestures, facial reactions and responses flow spontaneously and abundantly. The facial expressions in color slides of our hootenannies show, even without the music, the delicious savoring of what we are doing together. Even though we know all the funny lines—or perhaps especially *because* we know them—the children's faces alight with anticipation as they sing:

> If you like spaghetti
> All covered with cheese
> Hold on to your meatball
> And don't ever sneeze!

Then the room resounds with a loud *katchoo* followed by gales of laughter in appreciation of their own joke.

When we sing:

> If you're happy and you know it
> Hold your breath.

Within seconds the room is filled with merry giggles that hardly allow for earnest breath-holding but shows how much we are enjoying each other.

Arts and crafts opportunities abound in our classrooms. There are materials for tempera painting, finger painting, drawing, collaging, cutting, stapling, pasting, sawing, hammering, gluing, clay play, and print-making.

We provide a wide range of materials including not only the usual conventional ones but a wide choice of found ones as well. We often joke about this. Our madness, however, has method. We seek to encourage children to freely use a variety of conventional materials and also to experiment with new and different ones.

After hearing many discussions about children's art, I'm convinced much misunderstanding abounds. Some of it stems from too narrow a viewpoint. Simply because the materials used are art supplies, the end result does not have to be a work of art. I, for one, would be greatly pleased to see a child make constant use of these materials whether he produced art or not. Manipulating a paint brush, crayon, pencil, scissors, hole puncher, or glue requires him to use his fingers with strength and dexterity. As he matures, he will need to develop small muscle skills for many purposes. This is one distinct value derived from use of these materials.

One small muscle skill is writing. Whatever development these materials provide for this skill is worthwhile. In many instances, you can trace the sequence of a child's progress from scribbles, to lines that move in distinct directions, to symbols, to designs, to representations.

Messing around with art materials helps a child discover, through tactile sensations, differences in textures and such qualities as hard, soft, stiff, flexible, and malleable. Such activities are especially effective if the teacher includes conversation to reinforce concepts. We also use touch and other sense experiences in our clue games.

Hammers, nails, saws, and found objects are excellent materials. Watching a child's first efforts with hammer and nails might lead one to believe he is incapable of hammering a nail into wood, but his struggles prove to be a good lesson on human aptitude. Within a short span of time he masters this skill. Sawing is similar. I hope someday to snap a picture of a child who has just made his first cut all the way through. I have seen it happen many times. His facial expression depicts complete satisfaction.

I have heard many lamentations over the stultification of children's works. I would be inclined to agree that this often happens: A well meaning adult, eager to see results that fit within his limited definition of achievement, is sometimes the culprit. We serve a

child far better if we do our best to provide continuing opportunities—encourage him to try what he will—enjoy his efforts—and allow him to find his own way. There will be ample time and opportunity for him to refine his skills later. His first efforts should help him feel comfortable with the materials, and he should be encouraged to experiment in using them in different ways and be motivated to move ahead.

It's fun to watch and listen as children do their art work. Some use two brushes as they paint at an easel. In these instances the brushes are usually held prehensile style, and colors are heavily scribbled onto and finally through the newsprint. Then there is the wall painting style in which a child methodically covers the entire paper with several layers of tempera. An intriguing variant of this style is that of the child who paints distinguishable objects and then covers them over. It doesn't take long to discover that many children paint a developing story, and as the story changes, they paint over what is already there.

A few really enjoy drips. As they paint, they watch for drips to begin. When one starts it is caught with the brush and worked around. Some children create fascinating designs this way. I recently watched one who first made an interconnecting lattice by working the drips and then filled each section with a different color.

Some people do not realize how much interaction there is in art activities. It is frequent and varied. Some children take the liberty of adding touches to other's works. At times, as two are painting side and side, they switch places to modify each other's work. Buddies often manage to do their painting together. This can be a twosome, threesome, foursome, or even moresome. Some modes typical of this camaraderie are:

A child delivers a running narrative as he paints. His buddies join in with comments. At times their remarks prompt additions to the work in progress.

Two friends paint at separate easels, alternately narrating about their own painting and commenting about each other's.

Two friends work side by side making thermofax copies of each other's works. By observing closely you can discern that in some instances one completely copies the other, but just as often you see them alternating as originator and copier.

One child works at an easel while his friend works at a table, and they talk about each other's works as they produce distinctly different projects.

Watching a child's eyes sometimes allows you to discern the source of his inspiration. Recently I watched through the observation window as a girl painted and noticed that she repeatedly turned to look at the wall on the opposite side of the room. My curiosity impelled me to walk into the classroom. Then I was able to see what she was looking at. Apparently another child's painting had caught her fancy, and she was making a copy. She happens to be adept at painting and capably produces original works with quick spontaneity, but in this instance she chose to copy.

The teachers make notations about the children's works when a child is heard describing them. There are children who habitually take their works to the teacher and instruct her to make descriptive notes or titles. Once two small diagonal streaks of fuchsia pro-voked Mrs. Gilbert's curiosity. She asked the highly articulate artist to tell her about his painting. "Those are airplanes and that's the jet stream," replied Tommy.

Tommy's mother told me of their conversation about his picture of a face that had an especially long line for a nose: "That's a man with a bird on his nose and he's laughing at it."

These two brief conversations give a picture of Tommy—a child who readily converses, is well in-formed, has a lively imagination, and delightful sense of humor. At this time his skill as a painter is not great, but his interest may allow this capacity to develop.

I overheard Mrs. Dean in conversation with Helen who was making a drawing with crayons and magic markers:

> Mrs. Dean: That looks interesting.
> Helen: This is my mommy looking at a man who fell in different colors of ice cream. And you know something? My mommy is right near the ice cream.
> Mrs. Dean: Does she like that kind of ice cream.
> Helen: Yeah.
> Mrs. Dean: I'll bet that's why you made it for her.
> Helen: Yeah. Guess what? This is yellow hair.
> Mrs. Dean: Does your mommy have yellow hair? (Helen shakes her head to answer no.)
> Mrs. Dean: Why did you make it yellow?
> Helen: Because the other color wasn't there.
> Mrs. Dean: What color is her hair?
> Helen: Black. (After a thoughtful pause) Do you wanta know the colors of the ice cream?
> Mrs. Dean: Yes.
> Helen: This is green. This is blue—and yellow—and red.

Mrs. Dean: I'll bet it's delicious.
Helen: My mommy likes ice cream.

The working modes of young children are multi-farious. One studies meticulously as he makes each stroke. Another works rapidly and spontaneously. For instance, Darcy, whose flow of works is consistently aesthetically pleasing, began with what looked like a house. Then as she was coloring it, she abruptly decided to paint each section a different color. She then made a series of strokes dividing the background. After subdividing these, she painted a different color in each section. This completed, she stepped back to admire her work. Another inspiration came to her. She dipped the brush in blue and flicked on speckles.

Pleased with the effect she repeated the process—this time with yellow. Satisfied, she released the clips and hung the painting on the drying rack, her hands leaving interesting smudges in the corners. With a happy look on her face she nonchalantly walked to the sink and tried in vain to clean her hands. They remained distinctly blue despite her vigorous rubbing.

Finger painting is great fun. I watch them start working first with fingers and moving into fine, sharp lines with nails, then creamy, cloudlike puffs with circular motions of open palms. Spurred by success at trying different parts of their hands, some of the bolder ones try their forearms. One discovered he could make interesting dotting effects by arching his fingers and pounding away like a concert pianist mounting a crescendo.

As all of this is going on, the teachers periodically stop by, drop an eight by ten piece of newsprint on a painting, and gently rub the back to transfer the image. The child then continues until he decides to change to another activity.

A child whose paintings tell a sequential story has a great time with finger paints. In several instances we've managed to catch successive parts of such a narrative. Lisa's finger painting developed in a six part sequence: (1) A circle, (2) Three dots and a curve made a smiling face, (3) A flower was added, (4) The sun came out, (5) Raindrops fell, and (6) The rain washed away face, flower, and sun.

chapter 12 ∘∘∘∘∘∘∘∘∘∘∘∘∘∘∘∘∘∘∘∘∘∘∘∘∘

The Prime
Classroom – the
∘∘∘∘∘∘∘∘Great Outdoors

> To see a world
>   in a grain of sand
> And a heaven in a wild flower;
> Hold infinity in the palm
>   of your hand,
> And eternity in an hour.
>
> William Blake [1]

The great outdoors receives scant attention from both parents and educators. It is the rare parent who takes a really good look at the outdoor facilities of my school. It is the rarest of rare parent who looks at them and discerns their significance. Some ask, "Do the children play outdoors?" Some ask, "Do they play outdoors in the winter?" Some ask, "How much time do they spend outdoors?" These questions usually come from parents who calculate the "amount of time spent in educating the child." And time outdoors is automatically subtracted as *play*.

Educators, who should know better, are even worse. I have visited hundreds of schools, and only a handful have had worthwhile outdoor facilities. That statement gains further impact if one realizes that the schools selected for visits were trying to do exciting things. More often than not exciting things *were* taking place *inside,* but *outside* was the same old flat playground equipped with swings, seesaws, monkey bars, and slides.

I have always loved nature. As my exposure to it has increased, that love has grown. Quite some time ago, I rejected the notion that man is capable of conquering nature and adopted the Indian belief that man is of nature, not outside it, and needs to learn to live in harmony with his surroundings. Perhaps that tells why I regard the great outdoors as the prime classroom and the small indoors as the adjunct.

Examples to emulate were few in number. I knew what I was trying to do and simply by trying, I moved in the right direction. I learned by mistakes and by successes. I read whatever material seemed relevant. When I found effective pieces, their bibliographical references usually led to other interesting material. By now I have an ample supply of books, pamphlets, and articles, and new ones are coming in a constant flow. Even as I write this, I find myself reflecting, with pleasant nostalgia, what wonderful fun it was to pursue these searches.

One excellent source of material is that written by Lady Allen of Hurtwood. She is the founder of the World Organization for Early Childhood Education. She has written a number of books and pamphlets on nursery education and also on landscape gardening. Her pamphlets describe what have come to be known as adventure playgrounds. She tells about their origin in the pamphlet *New Playgrounds:*

The inspiration came from Denmark where the Emdrup playground was opened in 1943, during the German occupation. Prof. C. T. Sorensen, the famous landscape architect, had made many beautiful playgrounds in the city but was impressed that the children seemed to prefer messing around in junk yards and building sites and developing their own brand of play with the waste objects they found there. With great imagination and courage he started the Emdrup waste material playground in a new housing estate outside Copenhagen.[2]

In 1965 Lady Allen delivered an address at a meeting sponsored by the United States National Committee for Early Childhood Education. Here is an excerpt that gives some of the rationale behind the adventure playgrounds:

Children seek access to a place where they can dig in the earth, build huts and dens with timber, use real tools, experiment with fire and water, take really great risks and learn to overcome them. They want a place where they can create and destroy, where they can build their own worlds, with their own skills, at their own time, and in their own way. In our built-up towns, they never find these opportunities. They're frustrated at every turn or tidied out of existence.

The streams are hidden in the sewers, the hills and mounds are bulldozed out and buried under concrete, and the trees, of course, are not for climbing.

Small children, especially the under-sixes, need

space and air and freedom, where they can test their limbs and develop their strengths, and where they can meet and make friends with children of their own ages . . .[3]

The local office of the Cooperative Extension of the U.S. Department of Agriculture has been another helping resource. About four years ago its helpfulness increased when Jack Focht was appointed Cooperative Extension Agent. In addition to knowledge, Mr. Focht brings to his work a zeal that obviously springs from a love of ecology. He has collaborated with the schools and other interested agencies in sponsoring a series of workshops for teachers and others who work with youth. I have attended several of these and learned much. His basic thesis is identical to mine. In my view one who hopes to see and learn as much as possible about the world in which we live, must first see and learn as much as possible about what is right under his nose. Here is the way Mr. Focht says it:

The starting point is the teacher's attitudes toward her school's surroundings. She must first draw a *magic circle* about her school and seek to find the bluebird of Maeterlinck's famous play inside that circle. She must teach her children to see ordinary, everyday things with new eyes. Her class must discover the treasures in their own backyards and realize that the best things in life are priceless and free. . . .

The object is not just to teach the principles of ecology and the facts of natural history, but to get kids to see where they live and to react to the beauty or ugliness of their environment. Finding scraps of nature between the cracks of city sidewalks or in the polished granite sides of buildings may be as important as a trip to the woods. The appreciation of natural beauty requires the elements of science as well as aesthetics; for any creature who dares assume intelligent responsibility for reshaping his environment must not only know the laws of ecology and the scientific method, but must also be responsive to poetry, architecture, and the rest of the arts.[4]

While walking with the surveyor who was doing the field work for our school site preparations I remarked, "I can see that a whole new education is about to begin." He was a man of about eighty who looked like Robert Frost. His reply indicated he understood my thinking and agreed, "This is why I chose this profession as my life's work." I could picture him tramping many fields those many years, finding his way through the brush to locate the precious markers and monuments that are the guarded secrets of the surveyor.

It had taken three years of patient searching to find the property for my school. It is located in the foothills of the Ramapos on the northwestern perimeter of Rockland County in the southern part of New York State. Its four acres form an L block. The base runs east to west along a main road and the arm runs north along the intersecting country road. A tributary steam of the Mahwah River flows along the southern boundary. It feeds the lake that covers the bottom acre. On the lake's northeast shore is our home, a restored pre-Revolutionary War farmhouse. The school, a contemporary structure, faces the country road in the middle of the upper section. The horizontal sweep of its building line parallels the road. It is perched midway up the hilly terrain, which rises more than fifty feet from the road to the rear wall. Behind the school hills rise steeply to form a natural bowl.

These hills serve the children in many ways. In clement seasons they challenge them to climb. The children readily take up the challenge. After they reach the top, they run down, exhilarated with glee. When the earth is warm and soft, one child may decide that rolling down is a better idea, and soon he is joined by others. They enjoy this so much that they do it again and again. I made a twenty-foot slide bed, set it into the hill, and put next to it a stairway made of railroad ties. They enjoy this addition and use it often, but it doesn't even place a close second to the hill itself. When the snow is on the ground, out come the flying saucers. Certainly no trip to outer space can match the thrill felt by a child as he makes a rapid descent atop this updated garbage can lid.

In all seasons the hills and foliage are in easy view of the children when they are indoors. We enhanced the natural attributes by adding varieties of bird houses and feeding stations. Each classroom has a feeder set on a window, which are much used in the winter. Often, in the middle of a hootenanny, I have stopped so that all of us can admire, without distracting them, the variety of winter birds feeding there.

Usually several heavy snowstorms cover the earth most of December, January, and February. For weeks we are confined indoors for all but an hour or two a week. Knowing the different kinds of fun snow provides adds an element of anticipation to those grey days. One such fun day occurred recently when Lawrence Hirsch, an elementary school principal, and I were visiting elementary schools. Several times during our visits I turned to Mr. Hirsch and lamented that nobody had taken a look outside. It was a magical day.

The barren trees wore glistening coats of icicles. Several different times we saw clusters of birches bent to the earth by ice and snow. I kept wondering out loud why nobody had at least thought of reading "Birches."

We finished our visits in the morning, and I extended an impromptu invitation to Mr. Hirsch to visit my school after lunch. We reached there at about two, and much to my delight, three classes were outdoors. One had taken a walk across the fields, the second was flying the hills on the saucers, and the third was giving its play area its first winter tryout. Some of the children were making patterns in the snow by falling backwards and flapping their arms. I remembered my own children played this game when they were that same age. They called it "angels" because that described the patterns they impressed in the snow.

As we walked around, I heard underfoot the crunch of the frozen crust of the previous snowfall. I called to the kids, and about ten came over to help me unravel the mystery of the crunchy sound. Then Mr. Hirsch noticed animal tracks, and again we played detective and deduced that a deer had recently run by. Mr. Hirsch is a talented musician, and his presence promised a special rare treat. His banjo and his special stock of folk songs had given us much fun once before. Even so, it was not easy to lure the children indoors for a hootenanny.

Experiences of past winters alert us to the special delights and opportunities they offer. We anticipate some ice skating if there is an extended cold snap. We have the opportunity to see how the streams look when they are almost frozen over. Sun and snow make a variety of sights and pleasures. We always make snowmen. Thawing days are special. Few streams can equal the kinds made by sun, mushy snow and curious children. It does get messy—but oh, what glorious messiness. Perhaps our enjoyment of winter and all other seasons results from our heeding the advice offered in Frost's "The Gift Outright"—by giving ourselves to the land we become the beneficiary of its many gifts.

The evolution of the turkey pen is a good example of how an outdoor classroom can develop. The previous owner had left a small ten by twelve foot pen with a gable roof, slightly higher than four feet at its peak. It had an earth floor. Chicken wire enclosed one side. The roof slats had lost all but a semblance of the cover.

We decided to convert it to a shed for outdoor blocks and wheel toys. I stripped off the remnants of the roof covering and the chicken wire, built a plank floor, and recovered the roof. The way the kids used it taught us several things. The blocks get lots of use. They are supplemented by planks and milk crates so the children can make constructions large enough to climb upon and into. The amount of play and construction inside the shed and on its roof was far more than anticipated.

The roof is again full of holes, but this doesn't bother me. Climbing upon it and sliding off makes wonderful sense. This summer it will be properly repaired with plyscord under the roofing felt. Some ropes and ladders will be added, and slide boards will be accessible.

Watching the way children used the shed also helped us design the newest of our tree houses. It has an en-

closed downstairs room, an upstairs reached by a ladder and a slide for quick egress. The ins and outs, the ups, the downs, the overs, and especially the blocks, boxes, and planks that allow the girls and boys opportunities to build and manipulate space to their desires make these excellent play things.

As the above description implies, equipment is selected to satisfy the needs of the children. Their growth and development can be greatly enhanced if provision is made for play opportunities that allow them to run, jump, stretch, lift, balance, judge, and climb. The hills are, of course, for climbing, and they are given much varied use. Trees are also used. One of them, a low growing apple tree, often has a cluster of kids in its branches. As I pass by, it reminds me of the story *Caps for Sale* [5] in which monkeys steal a peddler's caps and make off with them into a tree as he dozes leaning against the trunk. I expect one day to read the children the story as they perch up there and act out the roles of the monkeys. A felled tree is another good climber. I have seen about eight kids lined up from the trunk on to an extended branch, pleased with themselves because their combined weight allows them to make it spring up and down.

The tree houses provide not only for climbing up and sliding down, but for all sorts of imaginative play as well. Tire swings are suspended from the trees in each play area. These are far superior to the conventional

jaw breakers—and far more versatile. We also have a combination swing and go-around made of four tires bolted together and suspended from a thick branch. Our more conventional climbers include bridge-ladder combinations, a climbing house, and rope ladders. A large galvanized pipe set next to a sand box makes both a climber and a crawl-through. Another climber that provides for imaginative play is a two-car railroad. The engine is a stubby water tank with a cabin made of roofing boards. The second car is a larger water tank with a T-ladder made of galvanized pipe.

Each of my three playgrounds has a large sandbox with a water-play facility nearby. Materials for water play have evolved from galvanized tubs, to these plus a large old bathtub, to concrete pools, which are still evolving into a series of connecting pools of different shapes and sizes that will allow for a wide range of activities as water flows from the upper to lower sections and is then recirculated.

Painting, woodworking, and other crafts are provided for as well as table games. Easels are nailed to trees and drying lines extended conveniently in spider web style between low branches. Work tables and benches are also set in each area.

Our "magic circle" can be very small or it can extend beyond the horizon. Sometimes a group of us squat close to the ground to observe the first signs of new growth or to watch an ant carrying a large breadcrumb back to his colony. It is delightful to see a child's eyes open wide as he turns over a large rock and discovers worms. He excitedly summons his friends when he sees two insects locked in battle. We sometimes box in four square feet with lines of string, and several of our young explorers look and list the different things they find there.

We have sometimes played an interesting game with plastic toothpicks of different colors. The teacher shows the toothpicks and explains they will be make-believe insects that will be thrown into the grass in a boxed-off section two by six feet. The children stand around the outside and pretend they are birds, using thumb and index finger of one hand to imitate pecking. They are given three minutes to retrieve as many insects as they can. When the time is up, the teacher collects their insects. During the discussion, which is followed by another try at the same game, they discover that toothpicks whose colors most closely match the grass are the least frequently picked. This makes a good beginning lesson in adaptation.

We take many walks through the surrounding areas. To make the most of the walks within our grounds, we have been setting up nature trails. As the children use the trails they are encouraged to discover the sights, sounds, smells, touch, and tastes of nature—what Rachel Carson describes as "the sense of wonder."

The act of inducing a child to get into water exemplifies the nature of interaction between a child and the elements of his environment. Initial responses, which range from fearful to daring, usually dissolve in delight upon immersion. Introspection has frequently helped me identify special experiences worth providing the youngsters. The memory of wading in a stream on a summer day remains high in my recall of sensual delights. When I read that a stream "is more than just water on the move: it is water teeming with life, for the stream provides a seemingly endless variety of places where plants and animals can live." [6] That passage clinched my resolve to build a gently graded access bank that would add the stream to our nature paths and be another learning center in our outdoor classroom.

A precious resource would be wasted if we confined our storytime to the indoors. Anyone who has read a book beneath a shade tree on a balmy day will attest that this is the finest of settings. I remember that in my own schooldays the teacher who dared hold class outdoors was looked upon with scorn by administrators, and many students regarded it as a cop-out. Much the same attitudes prevail today. Distraction heads the list of reasons given for not holding classes outside. It would seem only fair to question the efficacy of studies that cannot be pursued in an idyllic setting.

One of my few poignant memories of the Second World War was an hour of serenity on a hilltop in Port Moresby as I lay on my blanket looking up at the night sky listening to "Eine Kleine Nachtmusik." The caress of a light breeze added to my sensual pleasure. At school, on a hot summer day, we do this same thing. The children readily lie down. Some even doze. *Nature & Make Believe* [7] has been played often during these sessions. It includes Herbert Donaldson's "Season Fantasies" and "Once Upon A Time Suite" and also selections by Greig, Tchaikovsky, Lisadov, Rimski-Korsakov, Torjussen, and Debussy. I confess I was surprised at the children's interest the first time I played the record—I had underestimated their good sense. They fully enjoy both music and respite.

There could hardly be a more appropriate setting in which to read the *Wonders of Nature* [8] or *A Tree Is Nice*. [9] In the latter Janice Udry gives a rather comprehensive description of a tree's qualities and uses. *Birds* [10] is a fine beginning book about some of the most familiar species. Knowing we shall have occasion to dig deeper, I have a backup of resource books in our parents'–teachers' library. These include, among others, several of the Peterson *Field Guides*. [11] Most of us find our interest piqued by curious facts about animals. Leonara and Arthur Hornblow co-authored a "Strangest Things" series [12] that does this well. Discoveries of animal homes are enhanced when we read books like *Where Do You Live* [13] and *Let's Find Out About Animal Homes*. [14]

Almost every summer we've had fun watching tadpoles mature into frogs. Several readings of *What Is a Frog* [15] give the children a good understanding of what is happening. This past summer I graded a bank to give the kids easy access to the stream. A good sequel to the frog experience is sitting on that bank and "reading" *A Boy, a Dog, and a Frog* [16] by Mercer Mayer. The reason for the quotation marks is this book's complete lack of text. To "read" it requires the children to make up their own story. The amusing illustrations give the clues. Their first "readings" are often starchily stilted, but with a little warming up, the story becomes more and more fun—and it is indeed an excellent reading experience.

Children's exploration of living and growing things

can be tremendous fun that leads to still more fun. We find ourselves spending a fair amount of time tracing to and from the beginning of things. Although I wax no enthusiasm for the gypsy moth, I do appreciate it when he obligingly displays each stage of his metamorphosis.

Seeds are a fascinating aspect of this study of beginnings. They come in many forms from tiny celandine, which looks like a miniaturized peapod, to chestnut, which looks menacing, to black walnut, which looks like something out of the Arabian Nights. It would be a shame if we didn't probe, examine, scrutinize under a magnifying glass, talk about, read about, and even sing about seeds since they are all around us. Watching some of the ways they propagate is fascinating.

Seldom have I seen a child who could resist playing a twirling game with maple seeds. The profligacy of dandelions is readily understood when one realizes that the seedballs that are not dispersed by the wind get plenty of help as curious children blow them on their way. The child who can resist the temptation of throwing thistles at his playmates is either timid or a saint. I've seen some timid ones but have not yet come across a saint.

During a visit to another school I had an interesting conversation with an eight-year-old girl who was doing a study of flower seeds. She had planted a variety and had listed a number of characteristics to be observed, including germination time, growth time, duration of bloom, flower height, and so on. She was interested in what she was doing and enjoyed telling me about it. I learned from what she told me but couldn't resist suggesting that she try planting some sunflower seeds.

Seeing their growth and ultimate size could not help but inspire wonder.

The wonders and pleasures of our outdoor experiences are always in my mind's eye as we explore the outdoors. Motivating the children to want to acquire at least a reasonable knowledge of living and growing things is also on my mind. It bothers me to know that my own understanding of such concepts as the balance of nature or ecosystems began in my middle years. It disturbs me more when I think of how many individuals go through life without a glimmer of understanding of their natural environment.

I am not alone in my concern. Here is what Arnold and Beatrice Chandler Gesell have said:

There is nothing new under the sun, but to childhood all is novelty. The most commonplace things teem with novelty.

Children are in a stage of sense experience when this warm glow of contact through eye and ear and touch may be transmitted into the life of spirit; when light, shadow, sound, motion, and touch weave a tangle of lovely associations around commonplace experiences and build up a deep appreciation of life and things. Thus the truths of nature become unconsciously associated with emotional response, which deepens and safeguards them. The child learns more through unconscious absorption than through didactic prescription, and in nature study daily contact with the beauty, motive, and unceasing effort everywhere shown by plant and animal gives an impulse to individual character and sets standards of behavior.

The child who stands on tiptoe to peep cautiously into the new-found bird's nest, who feels the velvety softness of growing things beneath his feet as he hunts out the tiny wild flowers in the spring, who sows his own garden seed and waits to see the first young green push its way through the dark, moist soil is building up a reverence for life, a sense of kinship with it, which will uphold him in his later and deeper understanding of its meaning.[17]

The "sense of kinship" the Gesells refer to is not dissimilar to Erickson's conception of identity.

The traditional psychoanalytic method, on the other hand, cannot quite grasp identity because it has not developed terms to conceptualize the environment. Certain habits of psychoanalytic theorizing, habits of designating the environment as "outer world" or "object world," cannot take account of the environment as a pervasive actuality. The German ethologists introduced the word "Umwelt" to denote not merely an environment which surrounds you, but which is also in you. And indeed, from the point of view of development, "former" environments are forever in us; and since we live in a continuous process of making the present "former" we never—not even as a newborn—meet any environment as a person who never had an environment. One methodological precondition, then, for grasping identity woud be a psychoanalysis sophisticated enough to include the environment; ...[18]

Seeking to find effective ways to help parents understand our outdoor classroom, I set up five workshop sessions in the spring of 1972. They were held while school was in session. To avoid intruding on the children's activities, my living room and porch were used as the meeting rooms. The first group met all day. It included seven mothers and three fathers. These parents served as leaders of the four succeeding half-day workshops.

In planning a workshop one should be clear about what he expects to accomplish. I sought to inspire more than merely instruct. I wanted to help the parents gain increased awareness of their environment and give them some ideas on how they could enjoy their natural surroundings together with their children.

I began the pilot session with a description of the whys and wherefores of our adventure playgrounds and nature trails. This led to a discussion on the values of these play areas as compared with more conventional ones.

One mother told of an experience that had begun a month before the workshop. She had called to ask whether I knew anything about pond construction because she had just purchased a home situated adjacent a swamp. After giving her some suggestions on possible sources of help, I suggested that before taking steps to make a pond, she learn something about swamps. I sent her one of our library books entitled *The Life of the Marsh* [19] and invited the family to accompany me on an Audubon Society hike through a sanctuary that included a marsh and a swamp. Soon they began to enjoy the swamp and had been promised help from their town in clearing away dumpings that were threatening to blight it.

After the discussion, we went outdoors, watched the children at play, walked the hill trail, and finished up in a classroom where I showed them supplementary resources as well as books and pamphlets available in our parents' library.

When the morning-session children left, we returned to my home for lunch. Everyone had brought a box lunch. Mrs. Gilbert supplied a surprise salad, coffee, and dessert. The salad consisted of tender spring dandelion greens with Caesar dressing. Despite its wide availability, only one or two had previously tasted dandelion greens, but everyone enjoyed them.

Jack Focht joined us in time for dessert. After lunch he discussed ways of helping children enjoy and learn about the outdoors. Then he took us for a walk around the pond. Before starting out, he asked each parent to collect small objects such as interesting rocks, lichens, pieces of bark, or dried flowers. When we returned to the porch, he gave each of us a small piece of clay and asked us to make a construction of the objects we had collected. One father was delighted, "Now I'll get a chance to show off the talent I developed when I worked for a florist after school."

Their constructions were all excellent. One mother became a celebrity in her neighborhood when she gave hers to teenage neighbors. They thought she was really "with it" because the central object of her construction was a praying mantis' egg sac they would watch hatch.

All of us came away from that session in a state of euphoria. The succeeding parent-led sessions were every bit as good. An excerpt from the letter of a mother who attended one of the latter sessions summarizes the feelings of many of us:

I was so proud of what I had made at "his" place that I felt excitement about showing it to him. Art is communication of an idea in a fresh, new way. I felt a sense of urgency to create a beautiful object of the materials I had collected.

There was communication of ideas on many levels today. I appreciate the time and effort put into the parents' meeting. Let me know if, in some way, I can help transmit this experience to other parents.

chapter 13 ∘∘∘∘∘∘∘∘∘∘∘∘∘∘∘∘∘∘∘∘∘∘∘∘∘∘∘∘∘

Children's
Responses to the
∘∘∘∘∘∘∘∘∘∘∘∘∘∘∘∘∘∘∘∘∘∘ Outdoors

Our adventure playgrounds, nature trails, and utilization of the outdoors do more than develop an appreciation of the environment, the passing seasons, and the wonders of growing plants and animals. They also help children develop self-confidence and awareness of others. Here are examples of some ways our outdoor classroom has well served several children.

○ HORACE, The Scaredy-Cat
His name wasn't really Horace, but I chose to call him that because his beginning at school must have been filled with imaginary horrors. His screams filled the air eight or nine times each day for the first week. Indoors he was relatively calm; outdoors he found things to fear at almost every turn. He first shrieked as his mother put him on the school bus; he stopped yelling the minute the bus pulled away.

Horace began school in the summer. In this session we stay outdoors most of the time. To allow for a full choice of play activities, we take out equipment that usually is kept in the indoor classrooms. This provides a better balance of play. (We do the same thing in the opposite way when we are shut in for long periods. Then we balance by trying to make extra indoor provision for active play.)

Birds and bees and other children provoked his next series of screams. Our setting abounds with plant and animal life, and we glory in it. When a child discovers worms under a rock, we let him pick up his new found treasure, and if he wishes, he is given a paper cup to take it home to mommy. Horace had no such desires, but his screams served as Geiger counters to let us know when something had been found.

He was equally uncomfortable at active play. Almost any threatening action of another child started him screeching.

His mother warned me that he had a fear of animals, but I wasn't fully prepared for the dimension of his fear.

We took our first field trip at the end of the second week to the Strawtown Dairy. This is an ideal beginning trip for young children. It is a small farm that has all of the facets of dairy farming within a relatively close area—cows, barns, silo, machinery, grazing fields, a processing and bottling plant, loading platform, and usually one or two small milk trucks.

Because Horace was so timid, I held his hand to give him needed reassurance as we walked around. We had moved no more than thirty feet away from the bus when Horace shrieked. It was a good one. It startled me. At first I couldn't imagine what was happening.

Children's Responses to the Outdoors ❧ 169

Then I calmly looked around following the direction of his terror-filled eyes. There, at a distance of some three hundred yards, cows were grazing. If I hadn't seen Horace in action the preceding weeks, I wouldn't have believed what was happening. Even at that remote distance, he was terrified by the cows. This made no sense. I tried to reassure him by gently saying, "I'm holding your hand. I wouldn't let anything hurt you!" I suppose he had heard that before from his parents. He quieted down. When he was sufficiently calm, we continued on. This time we moved about a hundred feet, and again he screeched and again I managed to reassure him. This time we made it to the milking barn. The sight of the cows so close was too much. Horace's howls were so shrill and so persistent that I was forced to retreat with him back to the bus.

Our work was clearly cut out for us. Because I had been aware of his fear of animals, I had put him in Mrs. Ghosio's class for the summer session. Her childhood on a farm had given her a love of living and growing things—and much knowledge of them as well. Her classroom contains a treasure trove of precious discoveries including beehives, wasp nests, bird nests, mosses, and dead tree limbs bedecked with beautiful bracket fungi. She effectively transmits her feeling for nature to the children. Before much time has passed, their natural desires to explore and discover are enhanced by her attitude and know-how. Seldom has a child spent a summer in her class without having some of this rub off onto him.

Horace was no exception. At first she had to hold back to let him become more at ease. Then she had to hold hands with him for support and reassurance. Gradually he moved. He became comfortable with his surroundings and his playmates.

The final field trip was to the Tolstoy Foundation Farm. This is one of the few large diversified farms left in this area. It has chickens, ducks, geese, herds of cows, several bulls, sometimes a calf, a whole section of pigpens, and flocks of sheep. Although it has good machinery, there are still many farmhands whom Countess Tolstoy employs to provide meaningful work for European refugees before they resettle elsewhere in the United States. There are also crops—wheatfields, cornfields, great big haystacks, and a section of grape arbors.

This time Horace had a wonderful day. Without coaxing, he joined a group that was looking at the inside of a hen house. Not once did he balk at anything. But the final touch was sheer magic. A swineherd, a gentle old man with a long flowing beard that had to come straight out of a book of fairytales, held a piglet for the children to pet. Despite my love of nature, I had no desire to pet the piglet. It had coarse bristles for hair, and its odor was pure stench. Without being asked, Horace walked up to the piglet and affectionately stroked its bristly, smelly hair.

Horace had indeed made it—but that is not the end of this vignette. In the next regular school year he continued to do well and by June his development and his achievements far exceeded our expectations. He had developed that lively curiosity we try to nurture. He showed interest in almost everything that went on in school. He moved readily into new experiences and tried new materials without hesitation. He excelled in block building, and his construction made of wood and findings were so interesting that we constantly asked him to leave some in school for display.

Horace overcame his terror of animals, yet adults must remember that children's fears, whether imaginary or warranted, are extremely real to them. Consider Leonore Klein's tale about *Brave Daniel*.[1]

"This is the story of a brave boy" who growled at a lion, captured a giant, put out seven fires in a day, and put his hand in a tiger's mouth. "The lion was in the zoo, of course." The giant was a giant butterfly. The seven fires were the candles on his birthday cake. The mouth of the tiger was in the stuffed head that was part of a decorative throw rug. *Brave Daniel* might be almost any child. The functions served by their imaginary lions and tigers are described by Selma H. Fraiberg in her book *The Magic Years*. She tells about her niece Jannie's Laughing Tiger:

At dinner that evening my niece did not take notice of me until I was about to sit down. "Watch out!" she cried. I rose quickly, suspecting a tack. "You were sitting on Laughing Tiger!" she said sternly. "I'm sorry. Now will you please ask him to get out of my chair." "You can go now, Laughing Tiger," said Jan. And this docile and obedient beast got up from the table and left the company without a murmur.

Laughing Tiger remained with us for several months. As far as I was ever able to tell, he led a solemn and uneventful life, with hardly anything to laugh about. He never demonstrated the ferocity of his species and gave no cause for alarm during his residence. He endured all the civilizing teachings of his mistress without rebelling or having a nervous breakdown. He obeyed all commands even when they were silly and contrary to his own interests. He was an irreproachable guest at the dinner table and a bulky but unobtrusive passenger in the family car. A few months after Jannie's third birthday he disappeared, and nobody missed him.

Now the time has come to ask, "Who *was* Laughing Tiger?" If we go way back to the beginning we find that Laughing Tiger was the direct descendant of the savage and ferocious beasts who disturb the sleep of small children. It is not a coincidence that Laughing Tiger sprang into existence at a time when Jannie was very much afraid of animals who could bite and might even eat up a little girl. Even the more harmless dogs of the neighborhood occasionally scared her. At such times she must have felt very small and helpless before the imagined danger. Now if you are very little and helpless before dangers, imaginary or real, there are not too many solutions handy, good solutions anyway. You could, for example, stay close to mother or daddy at all times and let them protect you. Some children do go through such clinging periods and are afraid to leave a parent's side. But that's not a good solution. Or you could avoid going outside because of the danger of an encounter with a wild beast, or you could avoid going to sleep in order not to encounter dream animals. Any of these solutions are poor solutions because they are based on avoidance, and the child is not using his own resources to deal with his imaginary dangers. (Instead he is increasing his dependency upon his parents.)

Now there is one place where you can meet a ferocious beast on your own terms and leave victorious. That place is the imagination. It is a matter of individual taste and preference whether the beast should be slain, maimed, banished or reformed, but no one needs to feel helpless in the presence of imaginary beasts when the imagination offers such solutions. . . .

Under ordinary circumstances, these practical experiences with invisible tigers, fought on home territory under the dining table, in the clothes closet, behind the couch, have a very good effect upon the mental health of children. Laughing Tiger was a very important factor in the eventual dissolution of Jan's animal fears. When he first made his appearance there was a noticeable improvement in this area. When he finally disappeared (and he was not replaced by any other animal), the fear of animals had largely subsided and it was evident that Jan no longer needed him. If we watch closely, we will see how the imaginary companions and enemies fade away at about the same time that the fear dissolves, which means that the child who has overcome his tigers in his play has learned to master his fear.[2]

Parents and teachers have roles to play in a child's attaining mastery of his fears. By exposing him to experiences that provide him firsthand opportunities to gain understanding of his environment, we help him to vanquish his imaginary beasts. As he explores, discovers, messes around with the common elements of earth and water, and manipulates space by building his own structures, he not only gains knowledge and the ability to use his own resources, but grows in his emotional capacities as well.

○ CASPER, *The Meek*
Casper expressed himself well. The tenor of his conversation was that of a little old man, "Jimmy is not con-

siderate of others. His selfishness aggravates me," was typical of the phrases that dropped from his lips. Mrs. Dean and I made an early guess that he conversed much with adults. Not long after this his parents and grandaunt Emily came to observe and confer. These were the other members of his household. They confirmed our guess. As we talked, I pictured them involved in conversations with Casper. Certain of his gestures and phrases were patterned after those of grandaunt Emily.

They, too, fretted about the other children's behavior. I responded by saying, "Casper is a delightful child. When he tells about his experiences, it is easy to discern the warmth of your family relationship and that you do many interesting things together. His intelligence, his reasonableness, and his gentleness are fine qualities. But it would be a mistake to forget that he is a child. He clearly avoids rough and tumble play. At such times he moves near Mrs. Dean or Mrs. Crandall. His outdoor play is characterized by this avoidance. The sandbox is the only place he seems secure, but when someone near him gets rambunctious, he gets up and moves toward his teacher."

My comments did not surprise Casper's family. They had made similar observations at home. I explained that he needed to gain confidence in his own abilities and that we had to encourage him to struggle through these situations. I did not mean he had to become a fighter—that would have been completely out of character. I felt that his responses were based on total reliance on the protective presence of adults. At the very least he could learn that this was often unnecessary.

As the months passed Casper improved. His outdoor

experiences seemed to advance his progress. At some point he began using the bridge-ladder climbers. He was not graceful. He reminded me of a middle-aged man doing Spartan-like exercises at a gym. As he persisted, he became more agile. Our walks and explorations were awakening interest in him.

About this time we took a trip to Dutch Gardens, one of our country landmarks. Down the hillside, below the Gardens, is a picnic grove beside an old mill stream. On arriving at the grove the kids sat at the tables for their snack of juice and cookies. Without any conversation, I took off my sneakers and socks and waded into the stream. Within moments I had lots of company. Dragonflies hovered nearby as if to see what our splashing was all about. Water bugs skimmed swiftly by. We spied a community of water striders and watched in fascination as they skated along the surface on their spider-like legs. The kids splashed and explored until it was time to go.

As we were drying and dressing, several intrepid explorers started climbing the steep hill. Before the teachers could stop them, I joined them, stationing myself to lend a hand to those who flagged as they neared the top. Their climbing styles were unorthodox, but most of them made it to the top. Their efforts left them caked with mud. Casper was a glorious sight. He was covered from head to toe. But watching him that day I saw a happy child splashing in the water, and when he climbed the hill (without assistance), his face was alight with an unrestrainable smile. No audible words were necessary—that smile said, "I climbed a mountain!"

A child needs to experience many moments like this.

Everyone needs a sense of adequacy, but to a child achievement is especially important. By age three he has acquired only the beginnings of knowledge and skills. As he tries to learn and to do, he learns from scratch and does so with untrained and unpracticed sensory and motor skills. The adult who effectively helps him knows this and appropriately appreciates the child's efforts.

Pain and pleasure—failure and success—have much impact on his learning. Pain and failure can help to some extent, but an excess of either may be too discouraging for him. The value of play for the young

child's learning experiences cannot be overestimated. One of the essences of play is its carefree, undemanding quality. If it becomes too exacting, we are wont to say *it is no longer play.* The great lattitude that allows for trying, experimenting, and messing around with no great concern over shortcomings, imperfections, or failing plus the wonderful joy of the *I-can-do-it* moments are what makes play the ideal media for the child's learning experiences.

My school neither turns lambs into lions nor lions into lambs. In Casper's instance he remained docile but gained confidence in his ability to solve some of his own problems. His antagonist, Joey, had an equally interesting experience.

○ JOEY, *The Hitter*
"I think I better tell you that Joey was expelled from day camp after only one week."

As she said this Mrs. Gross' voice revealed her discomfort. She continued, "The head counselor said he was appalled by his behavior. He never saw a child use his hands so much."

"Is he that way at home?" I asked.

"Not with our family. He's pretty rough with the neighborhood kids, but they're older than he, and they always pick on him."

We were talking about an exceptionally big three-year-old. This conversation took place during his intake conference.

When school began, Joey lived up to his advance notices. Though it may sound contradictory, he seemed gentle when he wasn't using his hands. As we watched him, we began to discern some pattern in his behavior. He never exactly began an altercation, but he was usually the first to use his hands. There was a marked difference between his indoor and outdoor play. He rarely fought indoors. His favorite play there was houseplay. He put on a tie and fedora and became "the daddy." He usually wore this outfit all during his indoor play, even when he painted or worked at puzzles.

Outdoors he had to be watched. He loved games of chase, but when another child began to act out a fight, Joey made it real. If a child tried to take something away from Joey, the object was likely to become a weapon to strike the offending child.

Our familiarity with the community helped us understand Joey. It confirmed that Mrs. Gross had given an accurate description of the way the children played in her neighborhood. I suspect the standard parental injunction there was, "Don't come home crying to me. If so and so hits you, you hit him back!" Joey was the youngest, but his size made him appear older. Even if he had worn a sign stating in large letters I AM ONLY THREE, it would have done no good.

The climate of our school play began to affect him. The level of his interest also reduced his involvement in conflicts. We gave Mrs. Gross the names of two classmates and suggested Joey and they visit in each others homes. I told her I felt that his fighting was learned in his neighborhood. It was commendable that he chose to meet situations himself rather than run to her. At school he was discovering he did not have to fight to solve conflicts. This was reinforced in his visits with his two classmates. He learned that he could talk out his differences with his playmates. He became gentle.

Again, I repeat, we did not make a lion into a lamb. Gentleness was a substantial facet of Joey's character from the very beginning. Although his first weeks were difficult, he was easily reached. At the end of his first month at school, Mrs. Gilbert asked me to schedule a conference with his parents. Our talk left us impressed that the relationship within the family was wholesome. Both mother and father spoke of their family experiences with warmth and understanding. Mr. Gross was a giant. His manner was gentle, and when he recounted Joey's misadventures in his neighborhood, tolerance and humor wove through the descriptions. I could understand Joey's daily routine with tie and fedora— the warmth of the father–son relationship was evident. Mrs. Gross commented, "Joey is an affectionate child. You would be surprised if you saw how wonderfully he plays with his little brother."

We were not really much surprised. We look for the best in each child, and Joey's friendliness and gentleness could be seen even when we had to watch apprehensively to be sure he didn't whack a playmate with a trowel.

Children usually have good awareness of appropriate situational behavior. Anyone who has seen a child use the presence of grandparents to take advantage of his parents would understand this. This awareness in part explained Joey's quick adjustment to nursery school. The teachers' presence imposed reasonable limits on roughhousing, but their intervention was necessary for only a short time. Our use of the outdoors was another factor. By seeing and using some of its potential in the teaching–learning process, we open up many options for a child. The proof of the worthwhileness of these options is demonstrated daily. Joey showed it when he started his explorations and came back with such treasures as a live inchworm, which he offered to let me hold.

chapter 14 ∞∞∞∞∞∞∞∞∞∞∞∞∞∞∞

∞∞∞∞∞∞∞∞∞∞∞∞∞∞∞∞∞∞∞∞∞∞∞ # Field Trips

As we move out and about the "magic circle" advo-
cated by Mr. Focht, we discover a community filled
with natural beauty, history, and many fine examples
of man's ingenuity.

The seasons provide the framework upon which we
build our trips. Summer, being the season for growth,
encourages us to seek out living and growing things.
We visit dairy, produce, and livestock farms, a children's zoo, a wildlife sanctuary, and lakeside and
mountain trails.

In autumn, our first trip is to one of the area's oldest
produce farms to see a display of decorated pumpkins,
including comic caricatures of the farmer, his wife,
their cows and horses, a witch flying a broomstick,
and the old devil himself climbing through a hedge of
dried cornstalks. We have fun comparing ourselves and
our dress to these comic counterparts. This trip relates

well to the *Pennies for UNICEF* project mentioned earlier and to the holidays of Thanksgiving and Succoth. The late blooming pumpkins, the clusters of dried cornstalks, and displays of gourds and Indian corn are typical signs of the autumn harvest. The proprietor graciously gives each child a delicious Macoun apple and picture postcard of the display.

We next visit a duck pond. As the ducks waddle up to the youngsters and take crackers right from their hands, the children squeal with delight. We have a provisional problem trying to keep the kids supplied so they can feed their hungry friends. Our fall color tour, which often takes us to the Stony Point Battlefield, allows us to view the beauty of the autumn panorama.

Spring usually includes, along with the flowers that bloom, a resumption of building. After being confined to our grounds most of the winter, we anticipate both spring and the building starts in the area by a trip to a sand and gravel pit. There we see large dump trucks, cement trucks, earth movers, front-end loaders, and diesel shovels. The pit we visit has a concrete plant, and we usually watch the front-end loaders measuring out the proportions of sand and gravel and dumping them in the chute that dispenses them and the cement into the mixer tanks of the trucks. This pit used to have a large conveyor belt that carried the raw truckloads of earth up to a series of sorting bins where the earth was separated into topsoil and stones of assorted sizes. My own favorite sight was that of the conveyor belt and the sorting process, but this machinery was often closed down during our visits, and it finally burned down. One year we made the trip four times, and not once was that system in operation. As if he sensed my disappointment, a child came to school the day of the last trip with a Tonka replica of a conveyor belt. By using that and a colander, I was able to demonstrate how the earth was carried up the belt to the sorters and separated into topsoil and stones of graded sizes.

The statement that a good picture is worth twenty thousand words makes sense to me. Better still, being on the scene far surpasses the effectiveness of a picture. This is why I cannot be content with only talking about the butcher, the baker, and the candlestick maker. To learn about their community, the kids need to get out and see it. Since they regard it through three-, four- or five-year-old eyes, I try to enable them to get a good view by sketching out details I think they will find interesting before a trip.

Even if they just have fun, the trips can be considered as having value. Some children are afraid to go to new and different places. We have helped many such children by watching them, talking with them, giving appropriate support, and continuing to expose them to new experiences.

After trips to the highway department or the sand and gravel pit, we look in books to learn more. The *ABC of Cars and Trucks* includes well articulated pictures of large vehicles and short descriptions.

The children's usual Show and Tell fare includes some Match Box or Tonka models. These are faithful replicas that allows them to examine and identify working parts and functions.

A story that coordinates perfectly with the sand and gravel pit trip is *Mike Mulligan and his Steam Shovel*.[2] What particularly reaches me is the message about the pride Mike Mulligan feels for his work. A little boy asks him, "Do you think you will finish by sundown?"

"Sure," said Mike, "if you stay and watch us. We always work better when someone is watching us."

Not unlike that little boy, we are likely to pull our buses off the road in the midst of a field trip so that we may watch earthmovers or other large construction machines at work.

Although we visit farms, we also do our own farming at school. We've managed to grow radishes, squash, carrots, tomatoes, and pumpkins, as well as a flower garden.

Part of our site was once apple and pear orchards. The kids are able to see the old fruit trees during the four seasons. They can eat the ripe fruit and process it. With dull knives they slice the apples and pears from the trees, plus purchased fruits, to make fruit salad. They also make applesauce. By letting apple and pear slices dry in the sun, they prepare the same dried fruit their mothers buy in packages at the store.

After the dairy farm visit, they make butter by passing a pint of heavy cream around the classroom and letting each child shake it. By the time it reaches the last child, it has become butter. We open the container and spread the contents on crackers. It is, of course, the creamiest, tastiest butter ever.

Experiences such as these help build a bond between a child and nature.

As I described our field trips at a parents' meeting, a parent skeptically queried, "Do the kids really understand what you're showing them?"

"I'm glad you asked me that," I replied, "because it's

an important question I often ask myself." My response to his query was based on two pieces of feedback.

The first came during a conference with Mrs. Young whose son, Avery, was the youngest child in his class. The conference was scheduled at the mother's request to check on Avery's progress. We shared information about his home and school experiences and agreed that he was doing well.

"He recently told me a story that puzzled me," said Mrs. Young. "He likes to watch the "Lassie" program on television. The other day he said he visited a farm and had seen Lassie and Timmy and cows and barns and machines that put milk in bottles and milk trucks. I can't figure out whether he imagined it or actually took such a trip."

"He did indeed take such a trip," I assured her.

The details of her description surprised me. I asked whether he had told her anything else.

"He said they had machines for milking the cows and tractors with wheels bigger than himself. He said they also had cats and horses and that there were birds' nests in the barn."

"The only inaccuracy in the entire description was the name of the dog. Even that could be easily understood because the dog was a collie and nobody made a point of telling his correct name to the children."

That Avery, the youngest child in the class, had observed so much was far beyond my expectations.

The second item of feedback came in a phone call from Mrs. Holcombe to tell me her son Kenny's comments on his trip to the highway department, "He described the large trucks, the snowplows, the bulldozers, and steamrollers. When I asked him how he knew so much about the machines, he said a man was trying to tell them how they worked. I asked him if the man knew all about them. 'No he didn't,' said Kenny, 'but Mrs. Gilbert did.' "

I could fully appreciate Kenny's interpretation. The man in his story was an engineer who was a most solicitous guide. He described the machines using technical terminology. The sandspreader, for example, was identified as a "centrifugal spreader." Mrs. Gilbert stood next to him. As such definitions were given, she quietly added, "This is the machine that spreads the salt and sand on the icy roads."

Evaluation is not only critical *of* but critical *to* good education. Feedback from a child, his parents and others is an important ingredient of evaluation. Several years ago a letter came from a parent who had sent two children to my school. An excerpt from it almost perfectly restates what we set out to do:

> . . . Both Mrs. Gilbert and Mrs. Rosenthal have given Jane and John a keen awareness of the world around them—a love for nature, and an appreciation of their environment . . .

Avery's description of the dairy farm underlines the importance of exposing children to appropriate open-ended learning experiences. Harkening back to Dewey's advice about joining symbol and experience, we build upon the children's trips with discussions, stories, songs, experiments, demonstrations and related play experiences.

When our new school was in the process of construction, we made many trips to watch it grow from a hole in the ground to its completion. Seeing how a wall is constructed may prod a child to try to discover the inside workings of other things.

By longtime practice I do much building in the classrooms, with children participating whenever possible. Their woodwork lumber is scavenged at building sites by a small group of kids and myself.

Their block play consistently shows carry-over from trip experiences. They built their own airport after the airport trip, their own zoos after the zoo trip, and their own farms after the farm trip. If we see a child build a multilevel parking facility, we make an educated guess that he has recently visited the city. It's worth remembering that children's inspiration may come from trips they took with their parents.

Their representational paintings and drawings are sometimes even more interesting than the originals. We sometimes make experience charts by mounting a series of their art works and printing their commentaries.

The Education Development Center [3] in Newton, Massachusetts, has innovated an interesting project called *Kids and Cameras*. We began trying it recently. During their trips the youngsters take pictures, which they develop and print in class. The prints are then mounted on a chart, and their comments are added to create another kind of experience chart.

Over the years we have taken color slides of many of our activities. These are organized and shown at parents' meetings to interpret visually what happens in our classrooms.

Parents' questions about the kids' ability to comprehend what they see during their trips is the typical reaction of many adults. Onlookers have frequently expressed their surprise at how well the children handle themselves on trips. Those of us who have traveled with them year after year have come to appreciate their capabilities. If teachers sensitively tune in to their interests, boys and girls respond with delightfully contagious excitement.

In 1965 a man named Robert Roth pioneered our area's first comprehensive outdoor classroom—the Lakeside Nature Center. With help from the Cooperative Extension, the Audubon Society, and other agencies concerned with ecology, Mr. Roth and teenage students of the Lakeside School created a series of nature trails on a forty-acre site.

I followed the progress of this nature center, and when the local papers announced it ready to be open to the public, I called to arrange a visit. When Mr. Roth heard the ages of our students, he wondered aloud whether they could benefit from a trip. I assured him that they could, and he was willing to try.

As we started along a trail, Mr. Roth stopped to pick some twigs from a black birch and asked, "Try chewing this. See if you can tell what it tastes like." The kids identified it as a chewing gum tree. The adults recognized its flavor as wintergreen.

Then he picked some twigs from a flowering dogwood and said, "This is what the Indians used for a toothbrush." An offer of golden toothbrushes could not have elicited a more enthusiastic response. With cleaner teeth we continued along the trail. He stopped at a sassafras tree, crushed several of its leaves, held them to his nostrils, and sniffed. His facial expression told of its fragrance. He then offered it to their noses.

We moved into a wooded area. He stopped to identify the familiar three leaf cluster of poison ivy and cautioned them to avoid it. As we neared a brook he pointed to dragonflies hovering near the stream and asked, "Can you figure out what they are doing?"

"Flying!" "Looking for something!" "Eating!" Their responses were all correct.

He plucked some of the leaves of the jewel weed to show clusters of insects on their undersides. He used this as an illustration of the balance of nature concept. He then suggested they find firm footing while he turned over some large flat rocks in the stream bed. They watched excitedly when a crayfish scurried out backwards from under one of them. He showed how the leaves of the jewel weed glistened when held underwater. They had to try this themselves.

We continued on and found ourselves in a forest grove. "Feel how soft the earth is under your feet. It's like a thick carpet." The trunk of a dead tree blocked our path. "What do you think happens to these old dead trees?" This question puzzled them. "Let me show you." As he said this, he dislodged a rotted section and showed how it crumpled in his hands. "You see, this tree is rotting. If you look carefully at the earth, you can see pieces of rotting leaves and branches. Do you know what makes this happen?" There were some tentative guesses about animals and insects. He told them they had the right idea and then reinforced their guesses by explaining that certain insects eat dead trees and plants. Pointing to one of nature's ingenious designs—a formation of bracket fungus—he added that these plants helped in the decaying process. "These plants suck the juices out of dead leaves and trees." He

showed them some toadstools: "These are in the same family. After the rain, you'll find many of them. They seem to spring up everywhere." Like a magician doing sleight of hand, he picked several puffy toadstools and squeezed them. The kids watched as the water poured forth and were surprised when his open hand revealed only a small crumpled fragment.

"What does this look like?" he asked as he pointed to a small waxy white plant. By consensus we agreed it looked like a pipe. "That's right. It is called indian pipe. Whenever I see it, I remember that once Indians lived in these forests. Maybe these plants grow here to remind us. If you look closely, you can see a small orange flower in the bowl. It looks just as though the Indian left it only a few minutes ago."

He suggested we spend a minute in silence listening to the sounds of the forest. We became aware of rustling leaves. An occasional scratching noise told us of the presence of small animals and birds. A babbling brook could be heard in the background. Car noises from the roads loudly intruded. The interplay of leaves and trees with rays of sunlight caught our eyes. Its beauty inspired a feeling of reverence. As if to remind us we were in class, an oven bird shrilly called—teacher, teacher, Teacher, TEACHER, TEACHER!

We continued our walk to the forest's scrubby edge. There we found a piece of galvanized pipe mounted on a stump. It served as a sighting device for woodpecker nests cut in an old tree some seventy feet away. After each child had a turn looking, we continued along a path cut through grasses as high as the children's heads. The path straightened as we neared our starting point. Something seemed to be saying "Home free!" We listened to that voice and spontaneously broke into a run—the kids' laughter joining the rushing sounds of the rustling grasses.

notes ○○

2 **1.** Virginia Lee Burton. *Katy and the Big Snow.* Boston: Houghton Mifflin, 1943.

2. Alvin Tresselt. *Hi Mr. Robin.* New York: Lothrop, Lee and Shepard, 1963.

3. Millicent E. Selsam. *All Kinds of Babies.* New York: Four Winds Press, 1968; pap., Scholastic, n.d.

4. May Garelick. *What's Inside?* Reading, Mass.: Addison Wesley, 1955; pap., Scholastic, 1968.

5. Millicent E. Selsam. *How Puppies Grow.* New York: Four Winds Press, 1972; pap., Scholastic, 1971.

6. SVE Educational Filmstrips. 1345, Diversay Parkway, Chicago, n.d.

7. Erik H. Erikson. *Childhood and Society.* New York: W. W. Norton, 1963, p. 155, pap.

3 **1.** This is a paraphrasing of a description given by Mrs. Jones in the keynote address at A Conference on Early Childhood Education held April 23, 1966, at Rockland Community College.

7 **1.** Pauline M. Moor. *A Blind Child, Too, Can Go to Nursery School.* New York: American Foundation for the Blind, 1962, p. 5.

8 **1.** Joseph Featherstone. *Schools Where Children Learn.* New York: Liveright, 1971, pp. 163–5.

2. New York State Department of Education. *Developing Mathematical Awareness in Prekindergarten Children.* Albany, n.d., pp. 2–3.

9 **1.** Charles Shaw. *It Looked Like Spilt Milk.* New York: Harper and Row, 1947.

2. Bruno Munari. *Who's There? Open the Door.* New York: World, 1957.

3. John Dewey. *The Child and the Curriculum.* Chicago: University of Chicago Press, 1968, pp. 24–5.

4. Janis May Udry. *Let's Be Enemies.* New York: Harper and Brothers, 1961; pap., Scholastic, n.d.

5. Dr. Suess. *Green Eggs and Ham.* New York: Beginner Books, 1960.

6. Retold by Arlene Mosel. *Tikki Tikki Tembo.* New York: Holt, Rinehart and Winston, 1968; pap., Scholastic, 1970.

7. Wanda Gag. *Millions of Cats.* New York: Coward-McCann, 1928.

8. Langston Hughes. *The Dream Keeper.* New York: Knopf, 1932.

9. Lillian Moore. *I Feel the Same Way.* New York: Atheneum, 1966; pap., Scholastic, 1968.

10. Jane Taylor. *First Poems of Childhood.* New York: Platt and Monk, 1967.

10 **1.** These are taken from evaluations made annually by the National Association for Better Broadcasting, 373 North Western Avenue, Los Angeles, Calif.

   2. Distributed by UNICEF, United Nations, New York, New York.

   3. Ann McGovern. *Little Wolf*. New York: Abelard-Schuman, 1965; pap., Scholastic, 1965.

   4. Taro Yashima. *Crow Boy*. New York: Viking, 1955; pap., Scholastic, 1970.

11 **1.** John Langstaff. *Over in the Meadow,* il. by Feodor Rojankovsky. New York: Harcourt, 1967.

   2. Ruth Crawford Seeger. *American Folk Songs for Children*. New York: Doubleday, 1948, p. 21.

   3. Ezra Jack Keats. *John Henry, An American Legend*. New York: Pantheon, 1965; pap., Scholastic, 1970.

   4. Narrated by Norman Rose. *Train to the Zoo*. New York: 225 Park Ave. South, Children's Record Guild, n.d.

   5. Erik H. Erikson. *Childhood and Society*. New York: W. W. Norton, 1963. pp. 209–10.

12 **1.** William Blake. "Auguries of Innocence." *Selected Prose and Poetry of William Blake*. New York: Random House, 1953, p. 90.

2. Lady Allen of Hurtwood. *New Playgrounds.* London: E. T. Heron, 1966, p. 9.

3. Lady Allen of Hurtwood. "Playgrounds," an address delivered May 5, 1965, at Guggenheim Museum Auditorium; sponsored by the United States National Committee for Early Childhood Education.

4. John D. Focht. *Draw a Magic Circle Around Your School.* New City, N.Y.: Rockland Country Cooperative Extension, 1969.

5. Esphyr Slobodkina. *Caps for Sale.* New York: Addison Wesley, n.d.; pap., Scholastic, 1968.

6. Robert L. Usinger. *The Life of Rivers and Streams.* New York: McGraw-Hill, 1967, p. 18.

7. *Nature and Make Believe.* Valhalla, N.Y.: Bowmar Records, 1962.

8. Jane Werner Watson. *Wonders of Nature.* New York: Golden Press, 1958.

9. Janice May Udry. *A Tree Is Nice.* New York: Harper and Row, 1956.

10. Jane Werner Watson. *Birds.* New York: Golden Press, 1958.

11. A series of field guides on birds, animals, insects, trees, shrubs, flowers, stones, etc., published by Houghton Mifflin.

12. A children's series that includes books on animals, birds, and fish—co-authored by Leonora and Arthur Hornblow and published by Random House.

13. Eva Know Evans. *Where do You Live?* New York: Golden Press, 1961.